Black Theology and Ideology

Deideological Dimensions
in the Theology of James H. Cone

Harry H. Singleton, III

A Michael Glazier Book

THE LITURGICAL PRESS
Collegeville, Minnesota

www.litpress.org

Cover design by David Manahan, o.s.b. Photo: James H. Cone. Photo credit: Charlotte Raymond.

The Scripture quotations are from the New Revised Standard Version Bible, Catholic edition, © 1989 by the Division of Christian Education of the National Council of Churches of Christ in the USA. Used by permission. All rights reserved.

1　　　2　　　3　　　4　　　5　　　6　　　7

Library of Congress Cataloging-in-Publication Data

Singleton, Harry H., 1965–
　　Black theology and ideology : deideological dimensions in the theology of James H. Cone / Harry H. Singleton III.
　　　p.　cm.
　　"A Michael Glazier book."
　　Includes bibliographical references and index.
　　ISBN 0-8146-5106-2 (alk. paper)
　　　1. Black theology. 2. Cone, James H.　I. Title.
　　BT82.7.S56 2002
　　230'.089'96—dc21　　　　　　　　　　　　　　　　　2001038237

In memory of

James "Pap" Alford
(1965–1983)

and

Barbara T. Christian
(1943–2000)

May each of your spirits dwell with me forever.

Contents

Preface

This book represents my first formal expression of a life-long struggle regarding the efficacy of Christian faith in effectuating human liberation. To be sure, this struggle began when I was growing up as the son of a Baptist minister in Conway, South Carolina, where frequent church attendance was considered as crucial to human existence as breathing! Cherry Hill Baptist Church was not unlike any other black Baptist church in the southern United States: a warm, affirming religious community whose affection for its youth was exceeded only by a highly demonstrative expression of faith testifying to the reality of God's grace in their lives. This atmosphere instilled in me a profound belief in the goodness of humanity and the potential for a more equitable and just society. More importantly, the Cherry Hill "ambiance" nurtured in me a "mustard seed" faith that continues to anchor and sustain me.

Not surprisingly, as the son of the pastor, I was expected to attend church every Sunday. Yet the more frequently I attended the more I was put in a serious theological quandary. In what could be termed a Bultmannian "pre-understanding," I "intuited" that something was missing from this expression of faith—something major and crucial! As I began to encounter with greater frequency the depravity of human relationships, particularly in regard to race and gender, yet encountering a faith community that made it a peripheral issue at best, I came to see the limitations of this expression of faith. In so doing my "intuition" evolved into an epiphany—the concern primarily for metaphysical and mystical communion and the preoccupation with the religious individual failed to take seriously the theological significance of the sociopolitical liberation of oppressed peoples in history.

Soon thereafter, my epiphany became a deep concern when I discovered that this expression of faith came to characterize formal worship and theological understanding in the black community in a far more ubiquitous way; an expression of faith that cannot only be characterized as being divorced from social reality, but also having an acute aversion to those faith expressions rooted in social responsibility. It frowned on radical black clergy's exhortations to avoid complacency and apathy and that Christian faith demands a radical discipleship that surpasses formal worship. A radical discipleship that constantly challenges the status quo in its creation of untoward human relationships. What I experienced instead was an expression of faith in which the more ethereal and spiritual—in other words, divorced from social reality—its emphasis, the more religiously authentic it was considered. This I found particularly mystifying given an African American history of earthly suffering. Thus my theological development began struggling with the question, How can a religious expression be so meaningful to an oppressed people yet be so silent regarding the transformation of its social reality?

This struggle continued as I matriculated to the University of South Carolina as a college student. It was there that Afro-American studies professor Willie Harriford introduced me to the speeches of Malcolm X. In particular, it was Malcolm's critique of white American Christianity that marked my initial exposure to the notion of "ideological suspicion" and provided me with the insight necessary for demystifying my struggle.

Malcolm's critique helped me to see that this "antithetical duality" between an oppressive social reality and a socially detached expression of faith was not unique to my context but symptomatic of most oppressor-oppressed contexts throughout the world. I came to realize that these contexts did not exist by accident but were systemically created by dominant classes, and by white society in America (supported by white theology and the white church), to maintain their privileged position in society. Thus, Malcolm's articulation of this antithetical duality answered the "what" of my theological quandary, and his linking it with the creation and perpetuation of white privilege answered the "why" of my theological quandary.

Although Malcolm's critique of white Christianity took root in me in immeasurable ways, I was not totally convinced that Christianity is "the white man's religion." I reasoned that no religious faith could "belong" to any one race of people and deduced that Malcolm was struggling more with white people's interpretation of Christian faith and its deleterious effects on the liberation of black humanity than with the faith itself. Thus, what was needed was not necessarily an abandonment of a religious faith (though I am not opposed to this), but rather *more liberating interpretations of all religious faiths.*

In light of this, I continued to search for an expression of Christian faith rooted in the black liberation struggle. After returning home from college, my father gave me two books that he thought would aid me in that search: James Cone's *Black Theology and Black Power* and *A Black Theology of Liberation*. Both works had a profound impact on me and represented what I had been "intuiting" regarding Christian faith from childhood—a radical interpretation of the gospel that made the liberation of black people from sociopolitical, Eurocentric oppression its point of departure.

The passion with which Malcolm spoke and Cone wrote soon took hold of me in "conversionist" proportions. It was then that the "hand of God" consciously touched my soul, compelling me in the footsteps of Cone to primarily express my ministerial vocation as a theologian.

With the desire to more formally pursue my theological "issues," I entered the Interdenominational Theological Center (ITC) in Atlanta, Georgia, where I had the pleasure of being taught and mentored by womanist theologian Jacquelyn Grant. Her constructive critiques of my work sharpened my intellectual acuity in unparalleled ways. Most importantly, it was Grant's encouragement, along with ethics professor Riggins Earl and Old Testament professor Temba Mafico, that was indispensable in my success at ITC and my preparation for doctoral studies.

After graduating from ITC, I entered the Graduate Theological Union (GTU) in Berkeley, California. Already firmly rooted in liberation theologies, Malcolm's critique and Cone's theology continued to be the conduits through which I filtered theological assertions. However, I was still in search of a theological perspective that would serve as the link between Malcolm's ideological critique of white Christianity and Cone's theology of liberation—a theological perspective that made ideological suspicion regarding theologies that have given divine sanction to human oppression his/her point of departure. After having read Arthur McGovern's *Liberation Theology and Its Critics: Towards an Assessment* for a doctoral seminar in liberation theology, I would find that link in the theology of Juan Luis Segundo. In particular, it was Segundo's appropriation of Marxist thought in critiquing theology in particular and the ideological superstructure in general and his method of deideologizing those ideologies used to justify the dehumanization of oppressed peoples that brought me full circle with Malcolm's critique. Further, it was Segundo's charge to liberation theologians outside Latin America to apply his principles to their context that brought me full circle with Cone's theology.

In this respect, I constructed a dissertation project that would integrate these concerns. Working under the topic "Dimensions of Deideologization in the Works of James H. Cone," I attempted to show that Segundo's method of deideologization, that is, the exposing of religio-political ideologies that have given divine sanction to human oppression and the construction of new theological presuppositions rooted in sociopolitical liberation, has the greatest ability to bring liberative potential to Christian faith. Further, I argued that Cone's theology is the best example of a theology that is in a process of deideologization in my American context. Thus, in synthesizing the methods of Segundo and Cone, I was equipped with both universal and particular dimensions of deideological hermeneutics. The former placed ultimate emphasis on the ideological critique of Christianity while the latter provided me with a formal expression as to how that ideological critique is expressed in my context. It is a reworking of that dissertation that I offer here.

Special thanks go out to the following institutions and persons: the University of California-Berkeley and Graduate Theological Union libraries for providing invaluable assistance in conducting my research for this project; my doctoral dissertation committee, Drs. George C. L. Cummings, Timothy F. Lull, and Barbara T. Christian, for rendering insightful comments regarding the manuscript and for challenging me without hindering me; my Benedict College "support group," Drs. Janeen Witty, George Devlin, and Peter Jackson, campus minister Rev. Glenn Prince, School of Arts and Sciences administrative assistant Ms. Dorothy Richardson, and my colleagues in the Social Sciences Department; my students at Benedict College who continue to show me every day the true meaning of perseverance; and my family, both nuclear and extended, that all had a hand in "crafting" this theologian.

Harry Singleton
Columbia, South Carolina
April 1, 2001

Introduction

Does the theology of James H. Cone bring liberative potential to faith? This book will analyze the theology of James H. Cone in light of Juan Luis Segundo's method for determining a truly liberative theology, that is, *the hermeneutic circle*. It is defined as follows:

> It is the continuing change in our interpretation of the Bible which is dictated by the continuing changes in our present-day reality, both individual and societal. And the circular nature of this interpretation stems from the fact that each new reality obliges us to interpret the word of God afresh, to change reality accordingly and then to go back and interpret the word of God again and so on.[1]

The hermeneutic circle represents Segundo's attempt to maximize theology's relevance to human history by creating a method that is applicable to varying historical contexts. This is significant, for Segundo, insofar as he recognizes that the nuances of oppression differ in each context. Therefore, a method that is applicable to varying contexts is indispensable for the full liberation of oppressed people.

The hermeneutic circle consists first of two preconditions:

> The first precondition is that the questions rising out of the present be rich enough, general enough, and basic enough to force us to change our customary conceptions of life, death, knowledge, society, politics, and the world in general. Only a change of this sort or at the very least a pervasive suspicion about our ideas and value judgments concerning those things, will enable us to reach the theological level and force theology to come back down to reality and ask itself new and decisive questions.[2]

The second precondition is connected to the first.

> If theology somehow assumes that it can respond to the new questions without changing its customary interpretation of the Scriptures, that immediately terminates the hermeneutic circle. Moreover, if our interpretation of Scripture

---

[1] Juan Luis Segundo, *The Liberation of Theology*, trans. John Drury (Maryknoll, N.Y.: Orbis Books, 1976) 8.

[2] Ibid., 8–9.

does not change along with the problems then the latter will go unanswered; or worse, they will receive old, conservative, unserviceable answers.[3]

If the theologian does not incorporate these two preconditions into her/his method, for Segundo, then its conservatism and therefore its irrelevance is inevitable. It will lack "any here-and-now criteria" and in so doing will become a pretext for approving the existing situation or for disapproving of it because it does not dovetail with guidelines and canons that are even more ancient and outdated.[4]

These two preconditions, for Segundo, yield four factors.

> Firstly, there is our way of experiencing reality which leads to ideological suspicion. Secondly, there is the application of our ideological suspicion to the ideological superstructure in general and theology in particular. Thirdly, there comes a new way of experiencing reality that leads us to exegetical suspicion, that is, to the suspicion that the prevailing interpretation of the Bible has not taken important pieces of data into account. Fourthly, we have our new hermeneutic, that is, our new way of interpreting the fountainhead of our faith (i.e. Scripture) with the new elements at our disposal.[5]

Segundo constructs the hermeneutic circle in response to the classical theological methodology of academic theology. It treats faith and revelation, according to Segundo, as "divine absolutes" without taking into account the historical relativity in which the human subject receives them and how it informs the content of both. In Segundo's view, academic theology operates on the naïve presupposition that the human subject can be a recipient of a purely divine revelation and a possessor of faith without either being conditioned by the historical vicissitudes or cultural context in which the subject finds her/himself. It further operates on the assumption, for Segundo, that the biblical message is exclusively a universal one and should not be "contextually manipulated."

However, Segundo argues that faith and revelation can never be ahistorical inasmuch as humans are historical, experiential beings, and that, therefore, such factors will be inescapable in the way we see the world and what we value. As such, Segundo sees these factors as necessarily governing the way in which we live our faith and receive our revelations. This means that Segundo sees the contextualization of theological reflection as an indispensable component in liberating humanity. Therefore, theological reflection does not begin with divine revelation and move to the world of human relationships, according to Segundo, but begins with one's particular historical context and then moves to divine revelation. In light of this,

---

[3] Ibid., 9.
[4] Ibid.
[5] Ibid.

Segundo contends that the word of God is not an eternally pure body of knowledge but is subject to the same ideological tendencies as other forms of knowledge. His suspicion is that anything and everything involving ideas, *including theology,* is intimately bound up with the existing social situation in at least an unconscious way.[6] Thus any relevant treatment of the word of God, in Segundo's judgment, must incorporate disciplines of historical concentration, such as general history, ancient languages, biblical theology, etc., in order to bridge the present with the past. In fact, Segundo sees this correlation between past and present to be the cornerstone of a legitimate liberation theology. He sees the failure to establish this correlation as being methodologically naïve inasmuch as it would eventually be reabsorbed by the deeper mechanisms of oppression—one of these being the tendency to incorporate the idiom of liberation into the prevailing language of the status quo.[7]

This tendency, for Segundo, is seen in a historical neutrality on the part of academic theology on issues that have created oppressor-oppressed contexts throughout the world. This neutrality has affected the theology of the Church, according to Segundo, such that it has assumed stances of impartiality, in other words, a "transcendent universalism," relative to sociopolitical power relationships. Segundo, however, sees this so-called impartiality on the part of both academic theology and the Church manifesting itself in a highly partial manner praxiologically. Segundo sees in these stances a tacit, if not outright, approval of the status quo in its unjust treatment of oppressed peoples. Therefore, in Segundo's view, this silence of academic theology and the Church is a non-neutral and highly partial stance in favor of the existing order and thus is an ideological weapon for maintaining that order.[8] Any viable liberation theology, according to Segundo, must first seek to liberate theology itself from its ideological ties with the status quo.

Such a liberation theology, for Segundo, is engaged in a process of deideologization, that is, exposing as ideologies the theological assertions that justify human domination and destroying their credibility through constructive critiques and the creation of new theological presuppositions rooted in liberation. It attempts to make theology relevant to the present situation by relating it to the past in such a way that it challenges the ideologies that have historically sanctioned human oppression as a means of transforming the present. But more importantly, for Segundo, and for the purposes of

---

[6] Ibid., 8.

[7] Ibid.

[8] Segundo does not provide the reader with any examples of these "neutral" stances on the part of academic theology and the Church and how it affects the poor of Latin America. As we shall see later, this will be a significant point in the examination of the weaknesses of Segundo's theological perspective.

this book, a theology that is in the process of deideologization is one that completes the hermeneutic circle and brings liberative potential to faith.

Thus, I will seek to show in this work that the theology of James Cone represents a theology that is, in fact, in the process of deideologization. I will do so by arguing that Cone's theology "completes" the hermeneutic circle of Juan Luis Segundo. This represents my thesis. In so doing, I will establish that Cone's theology brings liberative potential to faith.

The structure of this work is as follows: I will show that Cone's theology meets each stage of the hermeneutic circle by taking a chapter per stage, taking the first half of each chapter to illuminate the anti-black ideological assertions of white clergy and intellectuals and the last half of each chapter to show how Cone's theological presuppositions represent a new way of theologizing rooted in unmasking these ideological assertions and constructing new methodological presuppositions that effectively counter their impact in creating conditions of oppression.

In Chapter 1, titled "The Black Experience and the Emergence of Ideological Suspicion," I illuminate the ideological tenets of the theology of the slaveholding community and, in particular, its assertions that the African slave trade was ordained of God and that the slave possessed no epiphanic value. I further show how the fear of race amalgamation by whites provided the motivation for constructing segregationist ideologies. I go on to describe how the slave community responded to these assertions through what I term *an eschatological decision for black liberation* and the making of the black prophetic radical tradition. I conclude with Cone's treatment of revelation demonstrating Cone's recognition of the ideological nature of white theological treatments of revelation (i.e., the non-epiphanic value of the slave) and his response.

Chapter 2, titled "The Western Intellectual Tradition and Ideological Suspicion," chronicles the history of the ideological tendencies of the Western intellectual tradition, giving primary emphasis to the ideology of black inferiority aesthetically, culturally, and intellectually. I next analyze the anti-black sentiments of the Western intellectual tradition's most celebrated figures (Voltaire, Kant, Hume, Hegel, and Marx), showing in particular how, despite his revolutionary leanings, Marx saw the global expansion of African colonization as an indispensable component in the process of human freedom. I conclude the chapter by examining Cone's treatment of the Western theological tradition and his assertion that, given the acutely anti-black nature of the Western tradition, (1) blackness must be the necessary starting point for relevant theological reflection and (2) because Jesus identifies with the oppressed and participates in their liberation struggle, Black Theology is Christian theology.

Chapter 3, "Hermeneutical Methodology and the Emergence of Exegetical Suspicion," examines the hermeneutical methodology of white religionists and theologians that departs from the ideology of the biblical legitimacy of black enslavement. I elaborate on the emergence of exegetical suspicion in Cone, that is, demonstrating his recognition that "the Bible has not taken important pieces of data into account," by examining his hermeneutical methodology in general and his treatment of the Exodus narrative and the Christ-event in particular.

In Chapter 4, "A New Hermeneutic," I take Cone's "new way of interpreting the fountainhead of our faith," "blackness as the symbol of oppression and of the certainty of liberation," and show how this new hermeneutic is developed in his treatment of the doctrines of God, humanity, Christ, eschatology, and violence and revolution. I evidence that Cone uses this hermeneutic as the basis for arguing dialectally that blackness is what the world means by oppression but what the gospel means by liberation. I further demonstrate that, from a pragmatic standpoint, this hermeneutic establishes an inextricable link between black strivings to liberate themselves from white oppression and the gospel of Jesus Christ.

Further, each chapter ends with a concluding section reviewing what was covered in the chapter and the reasons Cone's theology passes that particular stage of the hermeneutic circle.

Chapter 5, "The Case for Indigenous Deideologization," serves as my attempt to construct a viable theological method rooted in a synthesis of the methods of Cone and Segundo wherein Cone provides the particular dimension of the method (the black-white encounter in America) and Segundo provides the universal dimension of the method (the hermeneutic circle). Moreover, indigenous deideologization moves beyond academic theology to the voices of indigenous peoples and how Cone and Segundo incorporate their experiences into their theological perspectives. Thus, I seek to establish that any liberative theological method must include the tools of the academy and indigenous voices if it is to make a dent in the ideological hardware of white supremacy.

By structuring the book in this way it affords me the opportunity to accomplish two objectives. First, it allows me to respond to Segundo's challenge to make his principles applicable to my context. In choosing a contextual figure like Cone, it allows me to merge Segundo's method with Cone's content. Second, it provides me with the opportunity to remain in close contact with the thought of Segundo. Although the principle sources will be from the work of Cone, Segundo's method will provide the foundation and structure of this work. As such, a thorough grounding in his theological project is of decisive import for a substantive deideological appropriation of Cone's work.

I chose Cone for two reasons. First, he was chosen by Segundo himself as a thinker whose theology was a representative example of the completion of the hermeneutic circle. I found Segundo's choice of Cone surprising given the fact that Segundo could have selected a theologian from his own context. More particularly, I found the selection of Cone interesting in light of the fact that his theology receives little respect in academic circles on the grounds that it is void of analytical substance. However, the genius of Cone for me is that he was able to weave a passionate language about black pain and suffering into an academic theology that at times is too analytical. My second reason for selecting Cone is that his work represents the most definitive statement of Black Theology—the tradition in which I have decided to root my theological work. In addition, the quantity of his work provides me with a plethora of sources beyond his major works with which to explore the deideologizing aspects of his thought.

My further ambition with this work will be to seek the development of theological language such that it is at once passionate and analytical. A theological perspective possessed of passion yet void of analysis is not intellectually respectable and offers little more than emotional exuberance to the liberation struggle. A theological perspective possessed of analysis but void of passion runs the theologian dangerously close to an intellectual objectivity that does not take into account the pain and suffering of the oppressed. As such, I contend that one can find these qualities in the passionate language of Cone and the analytical language of Segundo. This is not to suggest that Cone's work is not analytical and/or Segundo's work is not passionate. Rather, it is to say that each theologian's work is predominated by one over the other.

Finally, my intent with this work is to reestablish the significance of the theologian to recognize the link between inhuman treatment and an equally inhuman treatment of Christian faith that justifies that inhumanity if theological reflection is to be relevant in our time. For while it is true that Christianity has served as a phenomenon that has enhanced the quality of life for untold numbers of humans, it has also been the vehicle for motivating human beings to commit some of the more heinous crimes against humanity in the modern world. Thus it could be cogently argued that for every person Christianity has brought up "out of the muck and miry clay," it has sentenced the same number of persons to a social, economic, and political "dry bones in the valley," in its use as an ideological weapon in providing religious approval for relationships of human inequality. My hope with this work is that it makes a meaningful contribution to those "dry bones" eventually becoming an "exceedingly great army." Until that becomes a reality, religious ideologies that give explicit or implicit approval to the status quo will continue to be of decisive theological import.

CHAPTER 1

The Black Experience and the Emergence of Ideological Suspicion

The first stage of the hermeneutic circle requires that the theologian analyze his/her reality such that it produces an "ideological suspicion" regarding the religio-political ideologies of the dominant class in both creating and maintaining the status quo. Indeed, for Cone, the emergence of Black Theology cannot be understood without a concrete knowledge of the history that gave birth to it. You have to be black with a knowledge of the history of this country to know what America means to black people.[1] According to Cone, this requires not only a deep grounding in the ideology of white supremacy, but also the black response in general and that of the black prophetic radical tradition in particular. In this chapter, I will examine what Segundo calls "our way of experiencing reality," with both aspects in mind. First, I will examine the black experience as an existential encounter with white supremacy chronicling how whites justified the enslavement and segregation of blacks. Second, I will analyze the black experience as an eschatological decision for black liberation showing how the black radical tradition responded to the ideology of white supremacy and how this lead to the emergence of Black Theology. Third, I will expound on the black experience as the contemporary revelation of God moving directly into Cone's formal treatment of the doctrine.

The Black Experience as an Existential Encounter with White Supremacy

The black experience in America can be effectively described as an existential encounter with white supremacy. It began with the deportation of Africans to the "New World," and their indoctrination into what Kenneth Stampp called "the peculiar institution."[2] Further, whites were keenly aware

---

[1] James H. Cone, *A Black Theology of Liberation* (New York: Lippincott, 1970) 37.
[2] There are several excellent accounts of the history of black people in America. See Kenneth Stampp, *The Peculiar Institution: Slavery in the Ante-Bellum South* (New York: Vintage Books, 1956); Benjamin Quarles, *The Negro in the Making of*

that the "success" of the institution of slavery depended on their ability to theoretically justify the harsh treatment of black slaves. While the area of justification necessarily centered around the slave's anthropological nature, it has taken on three forms in the unfolding of American history.

The first stage is what I have termed *the pre-Christianized stage*, which runs roughly from 1619 to 1740. It conceived of the slave's anthropological nature as being what Riggins Earl refers to as the *soulless-body* or *naturalist type*.[3] Naturalists argued that slavery was not a violation of the human rights of blacks on the grounds that all human beings are possessed of a soul and since the slave had no soul then he/she was not human. Naturalists claimed to be scientific authorities of their day on the theory of creation and the human races, and they were intent on proving that the slave of African origin was inferior to white people, both mentally and physically.[4] According to C. Eric Lincoln:

> From the beginning, the Anglo-Americans considered the Blacks among them as beings of a lower order who, if they were human at all, were not human in the sense that white men were human. Hence, neither the blessings of liberty nor the comforts of heaven were considered to have any reference to Blacks. It was simply understood that "men" were *white* men, whether the context was social, political, religious, or general.[5]

Naturalists sought to prove black inferiority by classifying the slave with lower animals, particularly the orangutan. Samuel Cartwright, in his essay "Slavery in the Light of Ethnology," argued that "the typical negro's nervous system is modeled a little different from the Caucasian and somewhat like the orangutan."[6] According to Cartwright, the blacks' inferiority is clearly apparent in their physiological make-up:

America (New York: Macmillan, 1969); Lerone Bennett Jr., *Before the Mayflower: A History of Black America,* 4th ed. (Chicago: Johnson Publishing Company, 1969); John Hope Franklin, *From Slavery to Freedom: A History of Negro Americans,* 3rd ed. (New York: Knopf Publishing, 1967). For an excellent treatment of the Reconstruction years see Leon F. Litwack, *Been in the Storm So Long: The Aftermath of Slavery* (New York: Vintage Books, 1979). For an account of the post-Reconstruction years up to the early twentieth century, see Rayford W. Logan, *The Betrayal of the Negro* (New York: Macmillan, 1965). For the classic treatment of the phenomenon of Jim Crow laws see C. Vann Woodward, *The Strange Career of Jim Crow* (New York: Oxford University Press, 1966).

[3] Riggins R. Earl Jr., *Dark Symbols, Obscure Signs: God, Self and Community in the Slave Mind* (Maryknoll, N.Y.: Orbis Books, 1993) 5.

[4] Ibid., 11.

[5] C. Eric Lincoln, *Race, Religion, and the Continuing American Dilemma* (New York: Hill & Wang, 1984) 42.

[6] Taken from James O. Buswell III, *Slavery, Segregation, and Scripture* (Grand Rapids, Mich.: Eerdmans, 1964) 21.

> The occipital foramen, giving exit to the spinal cord . . . is so oblique as to form an angle of 30 degrees with the horizon . . . so to throw the head somewhat backward and the face upward. . . . Hence, from the obliquity of the head and the pelvis, the negro walks steadier with a weight on his head, as a pail of water, for instance, than without it; whereas the white man, with a weight on his head, has great difficulty in maintaining his center of gravity, owing to the occipital foramen forming no angle with the cranium, the pelvis, the spine, or the thighs—all forming a straight line from the crown of the head to the sole of the foot.[7]

Naturalists not only saw the physiological make-up of the slaves as a sign of their inferiority, but their hue as well. In fact, naturalists argued that the blackness of slaves' skin was an external confirmation of the corrupt nature of their souls.

> Whites were of the persuasion that physical blackness was a definite sign that slaves were created inferior by God. How else could the sable body of the slave be explained? What was even more evident was the fact that the external blackness of the body was thought to be indicative of the internal depravity of the soul.[8]

According to Albert Raboteau, this was another way of saying that the inferior dimension of the self was equally as inferior as its external dimension.[9]

This is to be contrasted with the naturalist claim that the transparent nature of white skin was/is an affirmation of the spiritual, intellectual, and physical superiority of white men and women. Most importantly though, it affirmed for the slaveholding community that whites were possessed of a soul and blacks were not.

This would prove to have acute theological significance. For naturalists reasoned that if slaves had no soul, it precluded them from receiving a divine revelation. According to Earl:

> It was thought that the African's dark skin signified the impossibility of God revealing anything through her or his soul. How would it have been possible for God's revelation in the soul to have been imaged in the ebony face of the slave? When compared to the soul of the white human being, it was concluded that the African American's black face had no epiphanic value.[10]

Clearly, the naturalist approach was to convince the slave that dependence on slave masters for instruction regarding "human" existence was

[7] Taken from ibid. More will be said about skull structure or phrenology in Chapter 2.

[8] Earl, *Dark Symbols*, 13.

[9] Ibid.

[10] Ibid. I discuss how Cone argues theologically that the black struggle for liberation is the point of departure for any relevant treatment of revelation in the modern world in the last section of this chapter.

divinely ordained by virtue of the "fact" that only he (the master) had epiphanic value. In South Carolina, the Society for the Advancement of Christianity published a tract which read, "No man or set of men in our day, unless they can produce a new revelation from Heaven, are entitled to pronounce slavery as wrong. Slavery as it exists at the present day is agreeable to the order of Divine providence."[11] Put another way, the naturalists' intent was to convince the slave to see them as a medium of revelation giving them the pedagogical authority to instruct the slave that, among other things, slavery is as natural as the laws of nature. According to Cartwright:

> The same ordinance which keeps the spheres in their orbits and holds the satellites in subordination to the planets, is the ordinance that subjects the negro race to the empire of the white man's will. Under that ordinance, our four millions of negroes are as unalterably bound to obey the white man's will, as the four satellites of Jupiter the superior magnetism of that planet.[12]

To be sure, the ideology of white supremacy had to do with neither God nor the slave but solely with the master. While it is true that the primary purpose of the African slave trade was economic, the reduction of blacks to the status of heathens served a cultural purpose in that it afforded whites in general and English culture in particular the opportunity to entertain the idea of its own perfection. This process of setting up whiteness and blackness as polar opposites and elevating whiteness in a manner inversely proportional to the devaluing of blackness is what I refer to as a *white supremacist politics of difference.* C. Eric Lincoln puts it this way: "The Englishman considered himself first, above all. And when he contemplated his own perfection, he saw the alleged heathenism of the Africans as but one aspect of a generalized disparity. They were beings apart. They were not merely black, they were black and heathen."[13] Winthrop Jordan accedes with Lincoln in explaining the white supremacist politics of difference:

> Heathenism was from the Anglo-Saxon's point of view not so much a specifically religious defect, but was one manifestation of a general refusal to measure up to proper standards, as a failure to be English. . . . Being Christian was not merely a matter of subscribing to certain doctrines; it was a quality inherent in oneself and one's society. It was interconnected with all the other attributes of normal and proper men.[14]

Thus being neither normal nor proper, blackness became not only the sign but the source of the slave's depraved condition. As such neither the humanity of the slaves nor their cultural expressions were respected by whites.

---

[11] Taken from Buswell, *Slavery, Segregation, and Scripture,* 29.
[12] Taken from ibid., 14–15.
[13] Lincoln, *Race, Religion, and the Continuing American Dilemma,* 29.
[14] Taken from ibid.

It was all a matter of the black [people's] depraved condition. Since he [she] was not an Englishman, his [her] importance and his [her] place in the Englishman's scheme of things was predetermined. From such a perspective, the Anglo-Saxon could scarcely be expected to develop a warm appreciation for the African's humanity, his [her] native religion, or his [her] capacity to benefit from Christian instruction.[15]

Despite its "effectiveness," the presupposition that the slave possessed no soul was coming under increasing criticism. Ecclesiastical bodies and missionary societies began to see the increasing slave population as fertile ground for the propagation of the gospel. Both sought to challenge the theretofore widespread conviction that Christianity was not intended for inferior races. It lead Bishop Berkley of London to remark, "An ancient antipathy to the Indians . . . together with an irrational contempt of the Blacks, as creatures of another species, who had no right to be instructed or admitted to the sacraments have proved a main obstacle to the conversion of these poor people."[16]

This leads us to the second stage of the ideology of white supremacy or what I have termed *the Christianized stage*, which runs from approximately 1740 to 1863 (emancipation). Riggins Earl refers to the slave's anthropological nature in this stage as the *bodiless-soul* or *ideal Christian master type*. This type conceives of the slave as having both a body and soul with only the soul being created in the image of God. However, it was the unchangeable blackness of the slave's body, which signified the demonic, that left the ideal Christian master type unwilling to assert theologically that the slave was made in the image of God.[17]

This typology was looked upon with skepticism by slaveholders who feared that (1) the conversion of the slave meant immediate manumission and (2) the saving of a black soul meant equality with whites. These fears were soon allayed by white religious leaders who assured slaveholders that their intent was not to free blacks from slavery but to bring the institution greater respectability by justifying it on theological grounds. In so doing, pro-slavery advocates saw a new typology regarding the slave's anthropological nature as being inescapable. This was done mainly by conceiving of freedom from bondage only in subjective ways and never socially, economically, and/or politically. Thus Bishop Berkley, while a proponent of slave conversion, was quite explicit as to its limits:

Christianity and the embracing of the Gospel does not make the least alteration in civil property, or in any of the duties which belong to civil relations; but in all these respects, it continues persons just in the same state as it found

[15] Ibid.
[16] Taken from Buswell, *Slavery, Segregation, and Scripture*, 26.
[17] Earl, *Dark Symbols*, 15.

them. The freedom which Christianity gives is a freedom from the bondage of sin and satan, and from the dominion of men's lusts and passions and inordinate desires; but as to their *outward condition,* whatever that was before, whether bond or free, their being baptized and becoming Christians, makes no manner of change in it.[18]

William Fleetwood, bishop of Asaph, echoed Berkley's sentiments by declaring that masters "are neither prohibited by the Laws of *God,* nor those of the *Land,* from keeping Christian slaves; their slaves are no more at Liberty after they are Baptized, than they were before. . . . The liberty of Christianity is entirely spiritual."[19]

Moreover, slaveholders fears subsided even more when convinced by white clergy that religious instruction made the slave a more efficient worker. The most prominent proponent of this philosophy was Cotton Mather.

> Appealing to their self-interest, he urged that Christianized blacks would make more efficient slaves. He also told masters that they need have no fear of losing their slaves on account of baptism, since Christianity contained no law forbidding servitude. Mather urged that masters were duty-bound to teach their bondsmen [slaves] "that it is GOD who has caused them to be *Servants,* and that they serve JESUS CHRIST, while they are at Work for their *Masters.*"[20]

Therefore, the saving of a black soul, a positive event normally, was effectively incorporated into the ideology of white supremacy insofar as it not only gave the slave no hope for earthly freedom but actually increased his/her market value.

> The blackness of the African slave's soul, of course, was not assigned a state of immutability since it was the theological conviction that Jesus' blood could make it "white as snow." Implied in this conviction was the idea that the soul of the slave, having been washed in the blood of Jesus, had the potential of being elevated on a spiritual level to a similar status with that of the master's soul in God's sight. That this could happen on a social and political level was thought to be an absolute improbability. Whites readily concluded that the dilemma of the external blackness of slaves' bodies gave them the right to be viceroys of slave's souls and ultimately the rulers of their bodies on earth. It was conceded that while the blood of Jesus could not change the blackness of the slave's body, it would transform the status of the slave's soul. This alone, it was thought, would improve the slave's market value.[21]

---

[18] Quoted in Buswell, *Slavery, Segregation, and Scripture,* 31.

[19] Quoted in H. Shelton Smith, *In His Image, but . . . Racism in Southern Religion, 1780–1910* (Durham, N.C.: Duke University Press, 1972) 9.

[20] Quoted in ibid., 5–6.

[21] Earl, *Dark Symbols,* 16.

The only reward given the slave was an eschatological reward in the hereafter to be given by God only on the condition that slaves serve their masters well on earth for it is God that ordained their enslavement. Reverend Thomas Bacon explains in a sermon preached to a congregation of Episcopal slaves: "Almighty God hath been pleased to make you slaves here, and to give you nothing but Labour and Poverty in this world. If you desire Freedom, serve the Lord here, and you shall be his [Freepersons] in Heaven hereafter."[22] Further, the slaves were made to believe that wrongs committed against masters were done against God Godself and therefore that God's will was synonymous with their enslavement. According to C. Eric Lincoln this was done in an attempt to convince the slaves of the reasonableness of their servitude.

> Christianity had already been accommodated to black pacification and control in the interest of the most abominable institution to ever challenge Christian morality. In consequence, that version of Christianity urged upon the slaves bore no "good news" beyond a legacy of toil, and no hope for rescue this side of Jordan. It was a religion that called them to work and to die for the doubtful aggrandizement of self-appointed Christian masters whose calculated manipulation of the faith was intended to so confuse the slave as to make his [her] dehumanization seem reasonable and inevitable.[23]

However, as time progressed, slavemasters' fears of converting slaves on the basis that they possessed souls would become well-founded. Growing antislavery literature in both the South and North concerning the incompatibility of the christianization of blacks and their continued enslavement as well as numerous insurrections from the slave community itself sounded the death knell for slavery as an institution.[24]

This leads us to the third stage of the ideology of white supremacy or what I have termed the *post-Emancipation stage* (1863–civil rights era). It conceives of the ex-slave's anthropological nature as being human but inherently inferior to that of whites. In light of this, it compelled whites to separate themselves from blacks and to justify it on theologico-anthropological, cultural, and scientific grounds. This would lay the foundation for segregation.

In his article "The Ideology of White Supremacy,"[25] James W. Vander Zanden identifies three major ideological premises that undergirded the segregationist position:

---

[22] Quoted in Smith, *In His Image, but,* 12.

[23] Lincoln, *Race, Religion, and the Continuing American Dilemma,* 34.

[24] See ch. 3 of Buswell, *Slavery, Segregation, and Scripture.*

[25] See Barry N. Schwartz and Robert Disch, eds., *White Racism: Its History, Pathology and Practice* (New York: Dell Publishing Company, 1970) 121–39.

(1) Segregation is part of the natural order and as such is eternally fixed;

(2) The black person is inferior to the white or, at the very least, is "different" from the white;

(3) The breakdown of segregation in any of its aspects will inevitably lead to racial amalgamation, resulting in a host of disastrous consequences.[26]

With the end of slavery and the inability to control the physical movement of blacks, whites became increasingly fearful about maintaining their "purity." Of the three premises cited above, by far the most prominent was that of amalgamation or race mixing. Just as Nazi racists believed that "each race on this earth represents an idea in the mind of God," so today the defenders of segregation evoke similar sanction for separation, imagining that "God in [God's] divine wisdom ordained that [humanity] should maintain a pure blood stream in his [or her] own race."[27]

Even as early as 1866, Jeremiah Jeter, a Baptist clergyman, voiced the sentiment of the white community when he asserted that "God had implanted in [humanity] an instinct which set apart blacks and whites, and that social mingling between them violated the divine plan, since such mingling would result in miscegenation and thus 'degrade our noble saxon race . . . to a race of degenerate mongrels.'"[28] Less than a decade later in 1873, Jeter reaffirmed his insistence on the necessity of segregation: "Social intercourse and intimacy between the races must lead to the blunting, if not extermination, of the instincts divinely implanted, and to the encouragement of intermarriages between the races and their ultimate amalgamation."[29]

Mongrelization was feared by whites who saw blacks as innately inferior. This served not only as a basis for keeping the races separate but also for barring blacks from major governing positions. According to George S. Sawyer, a prominent member of the Louisiana bar:

> The social, moral, and political, as well as the physical history of the negro race bears strong testimony against them; it furnishes the most undeniable proof of their mental inferiority. In no age or condition has the real negro shown a capacity to throw off the chains of barbarism and brutality that have long bound the nations of that race; or to rise above the common cloud of darkness that still broods over them.[30]

Concerning blacks' ability to govern, Roman Catholic priest Fr. Abram J. Ryan proclaimed: "This is a 'white man's Government,' and upon this doctrine future political contests must be fought until the question is finally and

---

[26] Ibid., 122.

[27] Quoted in Buswell, *Slavery, Segregation, and Scripture*, 55.

[28] Quoted in Smith, *In His Image, but*, 229.

[29] Ibid.

[30] James W. Vander Zanden, "The Ideology of White Supremacy," *White Racism: Its History, Pathology and Pratice*, ed. Barry N. Schwartz and Robert Disch (New York: Dell Publishing Company, 1970) 128.

irrevocably settled."[31] Blacks' alleged inability to govern was also attributed to an array of traits believed to be inherent in the race. These traits included unreliability, laziness, thriftlessness, immaturity, immorality, criminal inclination, ignorance, incapacity for sustained mental activity, and special susceptibility to certain diseases.[32]

The theme of inability to govern would be the ideological basis for the modern age of racial discrimination that permeates all major institutions in America and continues to have a pernicious effect on the fulfillment of black dreams and aspirations.

This represents a cursory analysis of the ideology of white supremacy. Let us now turn to the black response.

The Black Experience as an Eschatological Decision for Black Liberation

As early as 1774, slaves were declaring publicly and politically that Christianity and slavery were incompatible.[33] This means, for Cone, that black slaves made an eschatological decision for black liberation with the "intuitive" knowledge that Jesus Christ had not willed their eternal bondage but their freedom. Thus, in Cone's view, because of the vastly different social existences of whites and blacks, the latter came to know a Jesus quite different from the one who had willed them to be servants. Theologically, this means that black people (were) are prepared to live according to God's eschatological future as defined by the reality of Christ's presence in the social existence of oppressed people struggling for historical liberation.[34] This is the meaning of an eschatological decision for black liberation.

Black religion, then, emerged out of the slaves' experience of servitude trying to make sense out of a senseless reality using the Bible, hymns, and testimonies as sources. The Bible had greater significance insofar as it was the primary source for sanctioning their enslavement. The most widely used narrative was that of the curse on Ham.[35] However, in 1779, black slaves responded to both the theological and anthropological assertions of the slaveholding community in sharp disagreement:

[31] Quoted in Smith, *In His Image, but*, 253.

[32] Vander Zanden, "The Ideology of White Supremacy," 134.

[33] Albert J. Raboteau, *Slave Religion* (New York: Oxford University Press, 1978) 290.

[34] James H. Cone, *God of the Oppressed* (San Francisco: Harper & Row, 1975) 195.

[35] Also referred to as the Hamitic hypothesis, it holds that the sons of Noah, Shem, and Japheth and their children are to rule eternally over third son Ham and his lineage because Ham mocked his father Noah in Noah's nakedness. Ham is believed to be of African descent and Shem and Japheth of European descent. Thus, slavemasters concluded that African enslavement was divinely ordained. I will elaborate on this and other scriptural justifications for slavery in Chapter 3.

> We perceive by our own reflection, that we are endowed with the same facul-
> ties with our masters, and there is nothing that leads us to a belief, or suspi-
> cion, that we are any more obliged to serve them, than they us, and the more
> we consider this matter, the more we are convinced by our right (by the laws
> of nature and by the whole tenor of the Christian religion so far as we have
> been taught) to be free.[36]

This affirms that, contrary to claims of black religion being exclusively com-
pensatory, black slaves opted for a transformation of human relationships
on the basis that slavery and Christian faith were incompatible. Using Christ
rather than the Bible, James Cone reaffirms this assertion and its close link-
age to the notion of divine retribution in the theological consciousness of
the slave:

> Despite its misuse in the white community (even the devil is not prohibited
> from using God's name) the black community is convinced of the reality of
> Christ's presence and his total identification with the suffering of black
> people. They never believed that slavery was [God's] will; and therefore every
> time a white master came to his death, black people believed that it was the
> work of God inflicting [God's] judgment in recompense for the sufferings of
> [God's] people.[37]

According to Frederick Douglass, "Slaves knew enough of the orthodox theology of the time to consign all bad slaveholders to hell."[38] Further, a white
observer of slave life in Georgia remarks:

> They believe, and I have myself heard them assert the same, that in the life to
> come there will be white people and black people; but then the white people
> will be slaves and they shall have dominion over them. I never saw a negro a
> Universalist; for they all believe in a future retribution for their masters, from
> the hand of a just God.[39]

Slaves also condemned masters to hell, particularly those masters who
thought they were heaven bound. A story frequently told in slave quarters
was this one: "The master called the slave to his sick bed. 'Good-bye Jack; I
have a long journey to go; farewell.' 'Farewell massa! pleasant journey; you
soon be dere, massa—*all the way down hill!*'"[40]

White ministers represented the pinnacle of black contempt, for it was
they who formulated many of the theological arguments that legitimated
slavery. This account from William Humbert, a fugitive slave from Charleston, South Carolina, explains in greater detail:

[36] Quoted in George C. L. Cummings, *A Common Journey: Black Theology (USA)
and Latin American Liberation Theology* (Maryknoll, N.Y.: Orbis Books, 1993) 3.

[37] Cone, *A Black Theology of Liberation*, 78–9.

[38] Quoted in Raboteau, *Slave Religion*, 291.

[39] Quoted in ibid.

[40] Quoted in ibid., 292.

> I have seen a minister hand the sacraments to the deacons to give to the slaves, and, before the slaves had time to get home, living a great distance from the church, have seen one of the same deacons, acting as patrol, flog one of the brother members within two hours of administering the sacrament to him because he met the slave . . . without a passport, beyond the time allowed him to go home. My opinion of slavery is not a bit different now from what it was then; I always hated it from childhood. I looked on the conduct of the deacon with a feeling of revenge. I thought that a man who would administer the sacrament to a brother church member and flog him before he got home, ought not to live.[41]

This contempt for masters and the yearning for liberation was also reflected in black sayings such as "Everybody talkin' 'bout heaven ain't going to heaven," and songs like "Go Down Moses."[42]

While the theme of liberation as retribution played a key role in providing meaning and hope for oppressed slaves beyond history, it would be the theme of liberation as revolution that would provide meaning within history. Both would form the foundation of the black prophetic radical tradition.

This tradition has produced such notables as Frederick Douglass, Harriet Tubman, David Walker, Henry Garnet, Richard Allen, Henry M. Turner, Benjamin Mays, Martin King, and Malcolm X. The method of the black radical tradition is reflected in the words of Garnet:

> Let your motto be resistance! *resistance!* RESISTANCE! No oppressed people have ever secured their liberty without resistance. What kind of resistance you had better make you must decide by the circumstances that surround you, and according to the suggestion of expediency. Brethren, adieu! Trust in the living God. Labor for the peace of the human race, and remember that you are FOUR MILLIONS![43]

Indeed, resistance to white supremacy and the further degradation of black people represents the fundamental purpose of the black radical tradition. It could take the form of a scathing critique of white society such as David Walker's *Appeal*[44] or a form of direct action such as the Underground Railroad or the slave insurrections. In fact, in many cases it was the objective of the former to inspire the latter.

---

[41] Quoted in ibid., 293.

[42] For an excellent treatment of the use of song in the black liberation struggle see James H. Cone, *The Spirituals and the Blues: An Interpretation* (New York: Seabury Press, 1972).

[43] Quoted in Gayraud S. Wilmore, *Black Religion and Black Radicalism: An Interpretation of the Religious History of Afro-American People*, 2nd ed. (Maryknoll, N.Y.: Orbis Books, 1983) 94–5.

[44] *David Walker's Appeal, in Four Articles: Together with a Preamble, to the Coloured Citizens of the World, but in Particular, and Very Expressly, to Those of the United States*

Garnet's famous "Address to the Slaves of the United States," is, according to Gayraud S. Wilmore, "one of the boldest invitations to insurrection in the name of religion in the history of American slavery."[45] Garnet requested that the slaves entreat their masters one last time for their freedom or face catastrophic consequences:

> Tell them in language which they cannot misunderstand of the exceeding sinfulness of slavery and of a future judgment, and of the righteous retribution of an indignant God. Inform them that all you desire is FREEDOM, and that nothing else will suffice. Do this, and forever after cease to toil for the heartless tyrants, who give you no other reward but stripes and abuse. If they then commence work of death, they, and not you, will be responsible for the consequences. You had far better all die—die *immediately,* than live slaves, and entail your wretchedness upon your posterity.[46]

Further, in the same address, Garnet argues theologically for an inextricable link between redemption and bloodshed and anthropologically that a dead life is preferable to a life of death:

> If you would be free in this generation, here is your only hope. However much you and all of us may desire it, there is not much hope of redemption without the shedding of blood. If we must bleed, let it all come at once—rather die *[freepersons] than live to be slaves.* It is impossible, like the children of Israel, to make a grand exodus from the land of bondage. The Pharaohs are on both sides of the blood-red waters.[47]

Arguably, the most notable examples of slave defiance were the insurrections of Gabriel Prosser, Denmark Vesey, and Nat Turner.

Prosser's insurrection occurred as a slave on a plantation just outside Richmond, Virginia. A student of the Bible, particularly the prophetic books, Prosser believed that God sent him to the slave community to lead it to freedom. He saw in Judges 15:14-15, 20 (Samson slaying the Philistines with the jawbone of an ass), the inspiration for the destruction of slavery and "to institute on American soil what Toussaint [L'Ouverture] was able to create

---

of America: Third and Last Edition (Baltimore: Black Classics Press, 1993). First published in 1830. Considered by Wilmore to be the most devastating critique of Christianity since Voltaire's "Catechisme de l'honnete homme." Concerning freedom as a natural right and not a gift from slave masters, Walker writes: "Should tyrants take it into their heads to emancipate any of you, remember that your freedom is your natural right. You are [humans], as well as they, and instead of returning thanks to them for your freedom, return it to the Holy Ghost, who is your rightful owner. If they do not want to part with your labors, . . . and my word for it, that God Almighty, will break their strong band." Taken from Cone, *God of the Oppressed,* 139.

[45] Wilmore, *Black Religion and Black Radicalism,* 94.

[46] Quoted in ibid.

[47] Quoted in ibid.

in the Caribbean—a free black people established as a nation."[48] However, the insurrection failed when the plot was revealed to slavemasters. Prosser was arrested on September 24, 1800, and executed on October 7, 1800.

Vesey was a free leader in Charleston, South Carolina. Like Prosser, he was a student of Scripture. For Vesey, the Zechariah 14 and Joshua 6:9 passages were of acute significance. The former speaks of the day of Jehovah when God will organize nations against Jerusalem and take the city. The latter contains the Israelites' siege of Jericho. Both no doubt suggested to Vesey a correlation between the history of Israel and the existential reality of blacks. Denmark Vesey, with an intuitive sense of the mystical and a good grasp of Scripture, must have seen parallels between the children of Israel—after they crossed the Jordan and stood before the cities that barred their way into the Promised Land—and the situation of blacks.[49] Like Prosser, before the scheduled June 16, 1822, insurrection occurred, slavemasters were warned and on the night in question the city of Charleston was surrounded by militia and police. Vesey was sentenced to death and executed on July 2, 1822.

Turner was a Baptist preacher in Southampton, Virginia. Through his reading of Scripture, Turner discovered that the God of the Bible demanded justice, and to know God and God's Son Jesus Christ was to be set free from every power that dehumanizes and oppresses.[50] On the sign of a solar eclipse in February 1831, Turner was to begin his insurrection but fell ill. It would be August 21 at midnight, after having preached to a congregation, that Turner revealed that God had appointed that night for black people to be delivered from slavery. Turner and those assembled set out for his master's house, killing him, his wife, and five others. They seized as much ammunition as they could find and began to kill everything in sight. However, the marshaling of forces by slaveholding communities from near and far proved to be too formidable for Turner and his men. Turner was able to evade his pursuers for six weeks but was apprehended on October 30, 1831, and hanged on November 11, 1831.

With the passage of the Emancipation Proclamation and the advent of Reconstruction, blacks were faced with the task of engaging white racism as a so-called "free" people. To be sure, this white racism took on new forms, particularly legislatively. With the Supreme Court's ruling on *Plessy v. Ferguson* in 1896 making "separate but equal" the law of the land, blacks were now faced with responding to a white racism that proclaimed them free but placed them in conditions comparable to those of their enslavement.

Unfortunately, this new white racism was not met with an equal amount of resistance by the black church, but brought on what Wilmore refers to as

---

[48] Ibid., 54.
[49] See ibid., 58, for Wilmore's elaboration on these passages.
[50] Ibid., 64.

"the deradicalization of the black church." Several reasons are proffered as to why this deradicalization occurred. Two of those reasons are the following:

> First, the post-reconstruction era was characterized by a commitment to integration into "American society." Thus followed the tendency to downplay the black militant antiracist Christian tradition and turn to white Christianity for identity and association. Second, some black scholars have argued that rapid urbanization and the persistence of racism have also contributed to the process whereby the black church lost sight of its specific vocation as an instrument in the struggle for black liberation.[51]

James Cone argues that the black church's deradicalization was the result of a waning hope for societal liberation in light of the persistence of black suffering after the Civil War. What would result was the institutionalization of the black church and a withdrawal from societal issues germane to black progress.

> The persistence of black suffering after the Civil War caused the great majority of black ministers to withdraw from political engagement and to devote most of their time to strictly ecclesiastical matters. The themes of liberation, justice, hope, love, and suffering were interpreted to support their withdrawal from political struggle for justice. Love became the dominant emphasis with a focus on Jesus in terms of patience, humility, meekness, peacefulness, longsuffering, kindness, and charitableness.[52]

Though there were exceptions to this process of deradicalization on the part of the black church,[53] the earlier theme of resistance of the black prophetic radical tradition was effectively usurped with one of accommodation and pacification.[54]

With the black church no longer being a medium through which the black prophetic radical tradition could advance its agenda, the latter created other arenas with which to do so. The founding of the National Association

---

[51] Quoted in Cummings, *A Common Journey,* 7.

[52] James H. Cone, *Speaking the Truth: Ecumenism, Liberation and Black Theology* (Grand Rapids, Mich.: Eerdmans, 1986) 95.

[53] The most notable exceptions are Henry M. Turner and Reverdy C. Ransom, both bishops in the AME Church, and George Washington Woodbey, a Baptist minister and member of the Socialist Party. See ibid., 95–6.

[54] Without question, this mood of accommodation that became endemic to the black church was impacted highly by the philosophy of Booker T. Washington. This philosophy conceded the dispensation of social, economic, and political justice to whites and saw the most effective way of appropriating resources for black survival from whites as black people ingratiating themselves with whites rather than publicly criticizing them on the basis of that dispensation. According to Washington, "sensible Negroes understood 'that the agitation of questions of social equality is the extremest folly.'"

for the Advancement of Colored People (NAACP) in 1909, the National Urban League (NUL) in 1911, and the Congress of Racial Equality (CORE) in 1942 gave the black prophetic radical tradition a platform for taking up the cause of justice for blacks in America. James Cone rightly points out that these organizations were highly influenced by the "pre-Plessy" church concerning its themes of justice, hope, liberation, love, and suffering, and often called on the church for financial backing and office and meeting space. In fact, so close was the relationship between the NAACP and the church, many declared that "the black church is the NAACP on it knees."[55]

The emergence of civil rights organizations also provided an outlet for black clergy who were finding the black church's deradicalization increasingly difficult as well as giving a support base to radical black clergy who remained in their capacities as pastors while engaging the struggle.[56]

The black prophetic radical tradition would reach its defining moment in the post-Plessy era with the advent of the civil rights movement. Its most prominent spokesman was Martin Luther King Jr., a fourth-generation Baptist preacher. King was well trained, having earned his bachelor's degree from Morehouse College and his master's and Ph.D. degrees from Crozer Theological Seminary and Boston University respectively. It was during his education matriculation that King was exposed to and greatly influenced by the writings of Paul Tillich, Reinhold Niebuhr, and Walter Rauschenbusch, and the nonviolent direct action protest method of Gandhi. Although King was well educated, Cone points out that in times of crisis during the civil rights movement, King "turned to the God of black faith." King's place in the black prophetic radical tradition is seen in his effectively reinterpreting the themes of love, justice, liberation, hope, and redemptive suffering out of their deradicalized forms. Cone puts it in more specific terms:

> He took the democratic tradition of freedom and combined it with the biblical tradition of freedom, justice and liberation as found in the book of Exodus and the prophets. Then, he integrated both traditions with the New Testament idea of love and suffering as disclosed in Jesus' cross, and from all three, he developed a theology that was effective in challenging all Americans to create the beloved community in which all persons are equal.[57]

Further, King saw unmerited suffering as redemptive and inescapable in the process of liberation. More particularly, he saw nonviolent suffering as the basis upon which blacks would be liberated from feelings of bitterness and

---

[55] Quoted in Cone, *Speaking the Truth*, 97.

[56] Three such examples are Benjamin Mays, Howard Thurman, and Adam Clayton Powell. For Mays see *The Negro's God* (Boston: Chapman & Grimes, 1938). For Thurman see *Jesus and the Disinherited* (New York: Abingdon-Cokesbury Press, 1949). For Powell see *Marching Blacks* (New York: Dial Press, 1973).

[57] Cone, *Speaking the Truth*, 100.

inferiority and whites would be liberated from a feeling of superiority. Cone again explains: "Through nonviolent suffering . . . blacks would not only liberate themselves from the necessity of bitterness and feelings of inferiority towards whites but would also prick the conscience of whites and liberate them from a feeling of superiority."[58]

King's strategy of nonviolent direct action protest would be the dominant approach of the black radical community from 1955 (The Montgomery Bus Boycott) to 1963 (The March on Washington). At this point, however, King's method would be criticized by those in and out of the civil rights community. With King's failure in the North as well as the outbreak of riots in many major cities, blacks began to seriously question whether King's strategy actually pricked the moral conscience of whites. In fact, King's most severe critic, Malcolm X, actually questioned King's morality in advocating a philosophy that did not allow blacks to defend themselves in the face of white brutality.

Malcolm was a member of the Nation of Islam that, as a black nationalist organization, saw very little hope for a "beloved community" with whites and opted instead for black unity, self-defense, and self-love.

Arguably, Malcolm's most significant contribution to the struggle was his powerful critique of Christianity. He rejected it as the white man's religion, used by whites as a medium for perpetuating the ideology of white supremacy and inducing pacification and quietism in blacks. "Christianity is the white man's religion. The Holy Bible is in the white man's hands and his interpretations of it have been the greatest single ideological weapon for enslaving millions of non-white human beings."[59]

Malcolm's critique, along with the riots, would have a huge impact on radical black clergy and others in the civil rights community. That impact would manifest itself during James Meredith's "March Against Fear" in June 1966. It was there that Stokely Carmichael proclaimed the slogan "Black Power." Carmichael was a member of the Student Nonviolent Coordinating Committee (SNCC), a group of young activists who began to see King's method as an ineffective way to bring about substantive change for blacks. The black power movement not only forced radical black clergy to struggle with the sociopolitical oppression of blacks but, with its emphasis on African heritage, it also raised the conscience of radical black clergy concerning the religio-cultural oppression engendered by centuries of black internalization of Euro-American theology.

Thus the approach of black radical clergy was to seek a synthesis between the black power of Malcolm X and the Black Theology of Martin Luther King Jr. They formed an ad hoc committee (The National Commit-

---

[58] Ibid.
[59] Quoted in Cummings, *A Common Journey,* 11.

tee of Negro Churchmen and later The National Conference of Black Churchmen or NCBC) and published a statement on "Black Power." It was published in the *New York Times* on July 31, 1966. The following excerpt reflects the overall tenor of the statement:

> The fundamental distortion facing us in the controversy about "black power" is rooted in a gross imbalance of power and conscience between Negroes and white Americans. It is this distortion, mainly, which is responsible for the widespread, though often inarticulate, assumption that white people are justified in getting what they want through the use of power, but that Negro Americans must, either by nature or by circumstance, make their appeal only through conscience. As a result, the power of white men and the conscience of black men have both been corrupted. The power of white men is corrupted because it meets little meaningful resistance from Negroes to temper it and keep white men from aping God. The conscience of black men is corrupted because, having no power to implement the demands of conscience, the concern for justice is transmuted into a distorted form of love, which, in the absence of justice, becomes chaotic self-surrender. Powerlessness breeds a race of beggars.[60]

NCBC was clear that it did not condone violence but was also clear that black people's liberation was an idea whose time had come and that black power was indispensable in bringing it about.

On May 4, 1969, NCBC accepted James Foreman's "Black Manifesto," and in June of that same year issued a statement on Black Theology.[61] In that statement, NCBC introduced the concept of Black Theology and defined it as "a theology of black liberation. It seeks to plumb the condition of black people in the light of God's revelation in Jesus Christ so that the Black community can see that the gospel is commensurate with the achievement of black humanity."[62] The next task for radical black clergy was to bring its theology to formal systematic expression. A task that would belong to a young theologue by the name of James H. Cone.

The Black Experience as the Contemporary Revelation of God

In *A Black Theology of Liberation,* Cone's treatment of revelation departs from the methodological presupposition that Jesus' identification with the poor and helpless reveals God as a God of liberation, an identification that makes the cause of the oppressed God's cause. Since, for Cone, the oppressed in contemporary America are black people, then God is found in and among black people making their cause for liberation God's own cause

---

[60] James H. Cone and Gayraud S. Wilmore, eds., *Black Theology: A Documentary History, 1966–1979* (Maryknoll, N.Y.: Orbis Books, 1979) 23.

[61] Both Foreman's and the NCBC's statements are found in ibid.

[62] Ibid., 101.

out of God's grace and mercy. This is the meaning of the black experience as the contemporary revelation of God.

According to Cone, Jesus' identification with the oppressed and not with oppressors reveals that God acts in history seeking the eradication of oppression in all forms rather than its perpetuation. Regarding contemporary America, this means, for Cone, the destruction of ideologies of white supremacy that condone black oppression and the construction of new forms of thought that have "usability in the struggle for black liberation."

> In a situation like this, there is only one course of action for the black community, and that is to destroy the oppressors' definition of blackness by unraveling new meanings in old tales so that the past may emerge as an instrument of black liberation. If the oppressed are to preserve their personhood, they must create a new way of looking at history independent of the perspective of the oppressor.[63]

Cone's new way of looking at history is to identify white theology as the anti-Christ for its use of Christianity as a medium for black oppression rather than black liberation. It further means a definition of Christian theology that seeks to affirm the liberation of oppressed people.

> Christian theology is a theology of liberation. It is a *rational study of the being of God in the world in light of the existential situation of an oppressed community relating the forces of liberation to the essence of the gospel which is Jesus Christ.* This means that its sole reason for existence is to put into ordered speech the meaning of God's activity in the world, so that the community of the oppressed will recognize that their inner thrust for liberation is not only *consistent* with the gospel but *is* the gospel of Jesus Christ.[64]

Of particular import for us is the phrase "God's activity in the world." While Cone agrees with contemporary theology (that is, the academic theology of white theologians done mainly in the twentieth century) that "God's self-disclosure is the distinctive characteristic of divine revelation," he does not share contemporary theology's treatment of revelation as "the rational discovery of God's attributes," "assent to infallible biblical propositions," or "an aspect of human self-consciousness." Rather, revelation has to do with God himself (Godself) as God is in God's personal relationship with humanity, effecting God's divine will in our history.[65] This means, for Cone, that God is a God whose will is known in history and not speculative rational debates about God's attributes. Thus, in Cone's judgment, God is either known through "God's activity in the world," in other words, as a liberator of the oppressed, or God is a white racist.

[63] Cone, *A Black Theology of Liberation,* 39.
[64] Ibid., 17.
[65] Ibid., 90.

This means, according to Cone, that any relevant theology must never lose sight of the dialectical relationship that exists between biblical revelation and social existence such that the former is always the basis upon which the latter is analyzed. Cone sees the opposite as the methodology of white theology insofar as it sought to equate a social existence of enslavement with biblical revelation. The racist will accept the view of revelation which stresses the self-disclosure of God as long as the interpretation remains antibiblical and thus does not challenge his right to define the limits of black humanity.[66]

This is why Cone sees it as crucial to the theological task

> to define revelation in such a manner that the definition will, on the one hand, retain the essence of the biblical emphasis and, on the other, be relevant to the situation of oppressed black people. In the zeal to be biblical, we can not lose sight of the contemporary situation and what this situation means to the oppressed of the land. If we fail by ignoring the poor and unwanted, we become antibiblical.[67]

Therefore, Cone goes beyond revelation as simply a knowledge of God's self-disclosure to assert that because God's essence as revealed in Jesus Christ is one of liberation, "revelation is God's self-disclosure to [humanity] in a situation of liberation." To know God is to know of God's activity of liberation on behalf of the oppressed. God's revelation means liberation, an emancipation from the political, economic, and social structures of the society.[68]

For Cone, the self-disclosure of God to humanity in a situation of liberation represents the essence of biblical revelation. And more importantly, Cone maintains that because the plight of black people in America can be characterized as a situation of liberation, the black struggle for liberation and the essence of divine activity are synonymous.

> Jesus Christ is not a proposition, not a theological concept which merely exists in our heads. He is an event of liberation, a happening in the lives of oppressed people struggling for political freedom. Therefore, to know him is to encounter him in the history of the weak and the helpless. That is why it can be rightly said that there can be no knowledge of Jesus independent of the history and culture of the oppressed. It is impossible to interpret the Scripture correctly and thus understand Jesus aright unless the interpretation is done in the light of the consciousness of the oppressed in their struggle for liberation.[69]

---

[66] Ibid., 91.
[67] Ibid.
[68] Ibid.
[69] Cone, *God of the Oppressed*, 34.

To be sure, Cone's intent is to strike at the very core of white religio-political ideologies in their historical treatment of the gospel as sanctioning white superiority and black inferiority. Not only does Cone effectively do this, but he also shows that black strivings to liberate themselves from white oppression is consistent with God's own work. God not only reveals to the oppressed the divine right to break the chains by any means necessary, but also assures them that their work in their own liberation is God's own work.[70] Thus, Cone establishes that God's revelation is not white enslavement but black revolution against that enslavement. Revelation means Black Power, that is, the "complete emancipation of black people from white oppression by whatever means black people deem necessary."[71]

Therefore, God's revelation must always be seen, for Cone, as substantive engagement with the structures of black dehumanization rather than as white symbolic gestures that make no contribution to the amelioration of black pain and suffering.

> God's revelation has nothing to do with white suburban ministers admonishing their people to be nice to black people. It has nothing to do with voting for open occupancy or having a memorial service for Martin Luther King, Jr. God's revelation means a radical encounter with the structures of power which Martin King fought against to his death. It is what happens in a black ghetto when black people decide to strike against their enemies. In a word, God's revelation means liberation, nothing more, nothing less.[72]

Cone's assertion that revelation is liberation can be seen more clearly when we examine the dialectical relationship of faith and history. According to Cone, the distinctive characteristic of Christianity is that the God of the Bible is a God whose will is manifested through God's participation in human history. "That is why Christianity has been described as a historical religion. It is a religion which affirms that we know who God is by what [God] does in the historical events of [humanity]. In fact, there is no revelation of God without history. The two are inseparable."[73]

For Cone, this is still not sufficient. He understands that if left in the above form, revelation is still subject to an ideological manipulation that justifies human domination. Cone sees this as being tantamount to limiting the knowledge of God to God's self-disclosure in a universal way. One must go a step further, in Cone's view, and examine the particular history of which God revealed/reveals Godself. God chose to make Godself known to an oppressed people, and the nature of God's revelatory activity was syn-

---

[70] Cone, *A Black Theology of Liberation*, 91–2.
[71] Ibid., 92.
[72] Ibid.
[73] Ibid., 93.

onymous with their emancipation.[74] Cone sees Exodus 15:1b-3 as the scriptural basis for his assertion:

> I will sing to the Lord, for [God] has triumphed gloriously;
>   the horse and his rider [God] has thrown into the sea.
> The Lord is my strength and my song,
>   and [God] has become my salvation;
> this is my God, and I will praise [God],
>   my father's God, and I will exalt [God].
> The Lord is a [person] of war;
>   the Lord is [God's] name.[75]

This passage is significant for Cone in that it "debunks" white claims that the freedom of which the Bible speaks is entirely spiritual. Further, it shatters the notion of blacks being "drawers of water and hewers of wood" to whites throughout eternity. Most importantly though, it establishes that the biblical view of freedom speaks not only of a freedom "from the bondage of sin and satan," but also from the bondage of human enslavement. It is God making a covenant with oppressed Israel to be their God and for Israel to be God's people. Cone explains:

> In this passage, God's revelation means political emancipation which involves [God's] destruction of the enemy. In view of God's overwhelming defeat of the Egyptians, a covenant is made with Israel. The covenant is an expression of God's identification with Israel and [God's] will to be her God and she [God's] people. The entire history of Israel is a history of what God has done, is doing, and will do in moments of oppression.[76]

What God "will do in moments of oppression" is where Cone connects biblical revelation to the black experience in America. Just as God liberated Israel from Egyptian slavery in the Bible, so too will God liberate black people in America from sociopolitical Eurocentric oppression insofar as God continually reveals Godself in "moments of oppression." Therefore, the biblical witness reveals that God is a God that not only does not condone human enslavement but seeks to destroy the power of oppressors to enslave.

> To be sure, there is an absolutely distinctive character in revelation, but God has chosen not to apply the radical otherness of divine existence to the struggle of the oppressed for freedom but to the oppressors who make people unfree. God came and continues to come to destroy the oppressor's power to hold people in captivity.[77]

---

[74] Ibid., 93–4.

[75] Ibid., 94.

[76] Ibid.

[77] James H. Cone, "Black Theology and Ideology: A Response to My Respondents," *Union Seminary Quarterly Review* 31:1 (1975) 77.

Thus, revelation, according to Cone, is not only a revelation of God to the oppressed that their liberation is God's also but further that God comes to effectuate that liberation by destroying the ability of oppressors to oppress.

Because, for Cone, God "continues to come" to liberate the oppressed, it is of paramount significance that the theologian recognize (1) the inescapability of contextualization in theological reflection and (2) the sociopolitical oppression within the theologian's context. Only then, for Cone, will the theologian be able to depart from a place that is at once relevant to the oppressed and is an affirmation of the biblical witness concerning God's intention for humanity.

This is why Cone maintains that the task of theology

> is to show the significance of the oppressed's struggle against inhuman powers, relating the people's struggle to God's intention to set them free. The theologian must make the gospel clear in a particular context so that God's people will know that their struggle for freedom is [God's] struggle too. The victory over evil is certain because God [Godself] has taken up the cause of the oppressed, promising today what was promised to Israel while they were yet slaves in Egypt.[78]

In response to critics who contend that Cone is merely projecting human needs onto God rather than moving from God's revelation to human needs, Cone lifts up another Exodus passage in which God chooses Israel over the Egyptians.

> I have heard the groaning of the people of Israel whom the Egyptians hold in bondage and have remembered my covenant. Say therefore to the people of Israel, "I am the Lord, and I will bring you out from under the burdens of the Egyptians, and I will deliver you from their bondage, and I will redeem you with an outstretched arm and with great acts of judgment, and I will take you for my people, and I will be your God" (Exodus 6:5-7a).[79]

This is significant, for Cone, insofar as it not only shows that the black struggle as God's struggle is not a human projection, but also that God chose and continues to choose liberation from oppression as God's way of disclosure to humanity. "It is because we know that we can trust the promise of God that we also know that the oppressed will be fully liberated. Indeed, their present struggle for liberation is God [Godself] making real [God's] promise to set them free."[80]

According to Cone, though God reveals Godself in human history, "only the community of *faith* is able to perceive God's revelation." Faith, for Cone,

[78] Ibid.

[79] Ibid. See the above edition of the *Union Seminary Quarterly Review* for critiques of Cone's theology from both black and white theologians and Cone's response to those critiques.

[80] Ibid.

is that medium that allows humans to recognize God's revelatory acts in human history. Faith then is the existential recognition of a situation of oppression and a participation in God's liberation.[81] According to Cone, all humans are able to recognize a set of events that take an oppressed people from oppression to liberation, but only the community of faith is able to perceive these events as God's revelation.

> All [humans] could have seen the exodus of a small band of people from Egypt and their subsequent entering into the land of Canaan, thereby establishing themselves as a recognizable community from about the twelfth century B.C.; but only those with the faith of Israel would know that these events of liberation are the revelation of God [Godself]. They did not happen by chance, and neither can they be explained in terms of [humanity's] capabilities. The only explanation in the eyes of Israel is Yahweh . . . who saw their affliction in Egypt, took pity on them and set them free.[82]

Thus faith, in Cone's view, is that existential element that enables the community of faith to perceive their struggle as God's struggle and is therefore "the community's perception of their being and the willingness to fight against nonbeing." Cone then applies this to the history of black people not losing sight of the dialectic of biblical revelation and social existence. Noting figures from the black prophetic radical tradition, Cone raises the question:

> Is it really hard for us to believe that black examples of this would be Nat Turner, Denmark Vesey, and Malcolm X? These men represent the "soul" of blackness and what black people mean by black liberation. They are the black judges endowed with the spirit of Yahweh for the sole purpose of creating a spirit of freedom among their people.[83]

Indeed, for Cone, the understanding that God's self-disclosure to humanity is one of actively working to create a total dissatisfaction with human oppression is the very meaning of revelation.

Conclusion

Hence, we have come full circle. We began the chapter by examining the ideology of white supremacy that supported and maintained the enslavement and segregation of black people. Ideologies that centered around the innate inferiority of blacks such that the slave, rather with or without a soul, had no epiphanic value, giving the slaveholder the pedagogical authority to instruct the slave in matters both human and divine. We then examined the black response wherein the majority of the slave community saw slavery as incompatible with Christianity. We also saw the making of the black prophetic

---

[81] Cone, *A Black Theology of Liberation*, 95.
[82] Ibid.
[83] Ibid.

radical tradition that not only perceived blacks as having epiphanic value, but also viewed God's revelation and black strivings for freedom as synonymous. Last, we examined the doctrine of revelation in the theology of Cone in which he put in more formal terms that the revelation of God is not a speculative phenomenon confined solely to biblical history. Rather, God's revelation continually occurs in human history wherever there are oppressor-oppressed contexts actively working to destroy the power of oppressors and calling the oppressed to participate in that work.

For the purposes of this book, this means that Cone has experienced reality such that it (1) lead him to an ideological suspicion regarding the existence of black people and the ideologies constructed by whites to justify that existence, and (2) lead him to a new way of doing theology by recognizing the ideological nature of all theological reflection and by treating revelation as a contextual and historical phenomenon rooted in divine liberation, rather than as speculative and ahistorical. And because Cone accomplishes this, he passes the first stage of Segundo's hermeneutic circle.

CHAPTER 2

The Western Intellectual Tradition and Ideological Suspicion

The second stage of the hermeneutic circle requires that we apply our ideological suspicion to the entire ideological superstructure in general, that is, all institutions and authorities that participate in the perpetuation of racial, gender, and class hegemony by using their power and influence to theoretically justify human exploitation, and to theology in particular. It is here where Marx's influence on Segundo becomes apparent. Segundo saw in Marx's statement: the ruling ideas of each age have ever been the ideas of the ruling class,[1] the ideological basis for exposing the ideological superstructure and theology's role in it. One discovers that role, for Segundo, in Marx's presuppositions concerning religious ideologies. They are: (1) that each and every religious form has a specific plane in the ideological superstructure of a given age; (2) that the pervading religious forms of an age, including those accepted by the oppressed class, derive from the living experiences of the dominant classes; and (3) that the process of discovering this connection abets the revolutionary forces of the proletariat.[2]

For Black Theology, "discovering this connection" means an analysis not of the economic modes of production in a given historical epoch (Marx), but rather of the origin and development of racial categorization and its link to the black dehumanization that emerged from it. In light of this, I proceed with this chapter to show that Cone meets the second stage of the hermeneutic circle in the following manner. First, I trace the ideology of white supremacy in regard to the Western intellectual tradition in its cultural- aesthetic and anthropological stages and the modern racism that emerged from it. Second, I examine the role of the Western theological tradition in perpetuating the ideology of white supremacy, giving emphasis to the significance of contextualization in theological reflection. Third, I analyze how Black The-

---

[1] Juan Luis Segundo, *The Liberation of Theology,* trans. John Drury (Maryknoll, N.Y.: Orbis Books, 1976) 14.

[2] Ibid., 16.

ology engages in a process of deideologization relative to the Western intellectual/theological tradition by examining the necessity of a Black Theology and the interrelationship of Black Theology and Christian theology.

Western Intellectual Discourse and White Supremacy

In "A Genealogy of Modern Racism," chapter 2 of Cornel West's *Prophesy Deliverance,* the author argues that black dehumanization aesthetically, culturally, and intellectually continues to exist in the Western world's most prestigious centers of learning. Further, West argues that the doctrine of white supremacy is not an isolated phenomenon but is systemic and institutional at its core. According to West:

> The notion that black people are human beings is a relatively new discovery in the modern West. The idea of black equality in beauty, culture and intellectual capacity remains problematic and controversial within prestigious halls of learning and sophisticated intellectual circles. The Afro-American encounter with the modern world has been shaped first and foremost by the doctrine of white supremacy, which is embodied in institutional practices and enacted in everyday folkways under varying circumstances and evolving conditions.[3]

West seeks to show that the problem lies primarily not in the ideology of white supremacy per se, but in "the way in which the very structure of modern discourse *at its inception* produced forms of rationality, scientificity, and objectivity as well as aesthetic and cultural ideals which require the constitution of the idea of white supremacy."[4] This is so, for West, insofar as Western intellectual discourse is guided by a logic "in which the controlling metaphors, notions and categories of modern discourse produce and prohibit, develop and delimit, specific conceptions of truth and knowledge, beauty and character, so that certain ideas are rendered incomprehensible and unintelligible."[5] One such idea, for West, is that of black equality aesthetically, culturally, and intellectually.

West attributes this enduring principle of Western discourse to scientific authority undergirded by a fusion of Greek ocular metaphors, Cartesian notions, and classical ideals. This fusion, for West, created an atmosphere that promoted and encouraged "the activities of observing, comparing, measuring and ordering the physical characteristics of human bodies." In discovering differences in the physiological makeup of whites and blacks and being given to the notion of the perfection of white humanity aesthetically, culturally, and intellectually, the idea of black equality found no refuge in the Western intellectual mind.

[3] Cornel West, *Prophesy Deliverance! An Afro-American Revolutionary Christianity* (Philadelphia: Westminster Press, 1982) 47.
[4] Ibid.
[5] Ibid.

The creative fusion of scientific investigation, Cartesian epistemology, and classical ideals produced forms of rationality, scientificity, and objectivity which, though efficacious in the quest for truth and knowledge, prohibited the intelligibility and legitimacy of the idea of black equality in beauty, culture, and intellectual capacity. In fact, to "think" such an idea was to be deemed irrational, barbaric, or mad.[6]

West then traces modern racism through two stages. The first stage is what I have termed *the aesthetic-cultural stage*. It began with the Western revival of a classical antiquity rooted in the ideal of ordering and comparing observations or what West refers to as a "normative gaze."[7] It would be J. J. Winckelmann who, according to West, sought to establish Greek physical characteristics as the standard of beauty to which all humans must aspire. This West found particularly questionable given that Winckelmann "never set foot in Greece, and saw almost no original Greek art (only one exhibition of Greek art in Munich)[;] he viewed Greek beauty and culture as the ideal or standard against which to measure other peoples and cultures."[8]

West also points out that it is in this stage that more direct attacks on the humanity of nonwhites and blacks emerged.

> For example, in 1520 Paracelsus held that black and primitive peoples had a separate origin from Europeans. In 1591, Giordano Bruno made a similar claim, but had in mind principally Jews and Ethiopians. And Lucilio Vanini posited that Ethiopians had apes for ancestors and had once walked on all fours.[9]

The theory of the separate origin of the races would become particularly useful for pro-slavery advocates in nineteenth-century colonial America. Leading the way were Samuel G. Morton, M.D., of Philadelphia; Swiss-born Louis Agassiz of Harvard; Josiah C. Nott, M.D., of Mobile, Alabama; and George R. Gliddon, U.S. consul at Cairo.[10]

Morton put forth the separate origin theory in two works, *Crania Americana* and *Crania Aegyptiaca* in which he argued that archaeological discoveries in Egypt confirm "that the Negroes of ancient Egypt were definitely inferior to the Caucasians of that country. Their social status 'was the same that it is now; that of servants and slaves.'"[11]

In 1847, to the chagrin of orthodox clergymen in Charleston, South Carolina, Agassiz announced in a speech "that he believed in an indefinite

---

[6] Ibid., 48.

[7] Ibid., 53.

[8] Ibid., 54.

[9] Ibid.

[10] H. Shelton Smith, *In His Image, but . . . Racism in Southern Religion, 1780–1910* (Durham, N.C.: Duke University Press, 1972) 155.

[11] Ibid., 156.

number of original and distinctively created races of men *[sic]*." In an effort to harmonize his theory with the teaching of Genesis, he argued that Adam and Eve were not the progenitors of all races, but only of the white race.[12] Therefore, Agassiz believed blacks to be inferior to whites and urged whites to recognize "the real differences" between themselves and the blacks and refrain from treating them on terms of equality.[13]

Nott published two lectures arguing that blacks and whites originated in separate creations and that because blacks had a smaller skull and brain than whites, they were both morally and intellectually inferior and therefore that the intermixing of blacks and whites resulted in a deterioration of the latter.[14] Nott confirms West's contention of the illegitimacy of black equality in Western intellectual discourse by insisting on an unbridgeable gulf between the black and white races and further that the Caucasian was "the most perfect work of the Almighty" and "probably the true Adamic race, whose history is so dimly shadowed forth in the Pentateuch." On the other hand, "no Negro has ever yet invented an alphabet, however rude, or possessed the semblance of literature." It was thus "a capital error" for zealous church goers and sentimental philanthropists to think that education, even over a long period, would "expand the defective brains, develop the intellectual faculties of the Negro Races, and thus raise them *by degrees* to the full standard of excellence which belongs to the Caucasian Races."[15]

Gliddon, as consul to Cairo, made his contribution by furnishing Morton with a collection of Egyptian skulls for observation.[16]

According to West, this genealogy of racism in Western intellectual discourse can be traced to the classificatory category of race in natural history, in general, and to the means of classifying human bodies by François Bernier in 1684, in particular. This would lay the foundation for naturalist Carl Linnaeus's racial division of humanity. Linnaeus saw the human species as fixed in kind—as "immutable prototypes." For Linnaeus, there are four races: *Homo Europeans, Homo Asiaticus, Homo Afer,* and *Homo Americanus.* For West, Linnaeus, unfortunately, did not stop there. He engaged in a hierarchical ranking of races best illuminated by this comparison of the European and the African:

---

[12] Ibid., 157.

[13] Ibid.

[14] Ibid., 157–8. Moses Ashley Curtis of North Carolina, an Episcopal minister and botanist, challenged Nott's findings. He argued that the so-called distinctive marks of blacks, i.e., skull, arm, knee, and heel, could be found more or less in other races. He also challenged Nott's assertion that varieties in the human family were not affected by physical factors. See ibid., 158.

[15] Ibid., 160.

[16] Ibid., 155.

European. White, Sanguine, Brawny. Hair abundantly flowing. Eyes blue.
Gentle, acute, inventive. Covered with close vestments. Governed by customs.
African. Black, Phlegmatic, Relaxed. Hair black, frizzled. Skin silky. Nose
flat. Lips tumid. Women's bosom a matter of modesty. Breasts give milk abundantly. Crafty, indolent. Negligent. Anoints himself with grease. Governed by
caprice.[17]

This dualistic way of looking at black and white humanity leads us to the
second stage of the emergence of modern racism, what I have termed *the
anthropological stage.* For West, this stage is characterized by the rise of the
disciplines phrenology (the reading of skulls) and physiognomy (the reading of faces). These disciplines served as a complement to the aesthetic-
cultural stage, for West, in that they "acknowledged the European value-
laden character of their observations."

This period would begin with the discovery of the famous "facial angle"
by Dutch anatomist Pieter Camper. For Camper, the ideal "facial angle" was
a one-hundred-degree angle which was achieved only by the ancient
Greeks.[18] Thus, Camper buttresses Winckelmann's contention that Greek
physiological and anatomical characteristics were aesthetically perfect.
What would serve as a devastating factor in establishing black equality as a
legitimate form of Western intellectual discourse was Camper's equating of
perfect Greek characteristics with one's nature, character, and soul, and the
conclusion drawn about those who do not possess such characteristics:

> Camper held that a beautiful face, beautiful body, beautiful nature, beautiful
> character and beautiful soul were inseparable. He tried to show that the "fa-
> cial angle" of Europeans measured about 97 degrees and those of black people
> between 60 and 70 degrees, closer to the measurements of apes and dogs
> than to human beings.[19]

Thus, for Camper, since the angle of white skulls was closer to that of the
Greeks than blacks, it not only precluded the latter from recognition as
equal human beings, but because the difference in skull angle was so large,
it made blacks more akin to lower animals.

The physiognomy assault on black equality in Western intellectual discourse was lead, according to West, by Johann Kaspar Lavater. This new dis-
cipline linked particular visible characteristics of human bodies, especially
those of the face, to the character and capacities of human beings.[20] Like
Camper, Lavater saw "the classical ideals of beauty, proportion, and mod-
eration regulated the classifying and ranking of groups of human bodies."[21]

[17] West, *Prophesy Deliverance!* 56.
[18] Ibid., 58.
[19] Ibid.
[20] Ibid.
[21] Ibid.

He also held, as did Camper, that Greek features were the standard of beauty.

For West, Lavater's expression of the "normative gaze" no longer meant elaborate observation of racial differences but rather visual glances. Lavater thought that quick visualization allowed one to draw more substantive conclusions than detailed observations. Thus, West found it no strange surprise that "Lavater put forth an elaborate theory of noses, the most striking member of the face. Neither is it surprising that subsequent classification of noses, based on Lavater's formulations, associate Roman and Greek noses with conquerors and persons of refinement and taste."[22] Thus the idea of black equality in Western intellectual discourse was squelched by the presupposition of the superiority of European (and more particularly Greek) anatomical and physiological characteristics resulting in the supposition of white superiority aesthetically, culturally, and intellectually as the medium through which Western intellectual discourse prohibits and delimits the notion of black equality rendering it incomprehensible and unintelligible.

This intellectual legitimation of white supremacy would continue into the Enlightenment period, affecting even the most influential and celebrated thinkers of Western intellectual discourse. Aristotle had earlier laid the foundation with his ontological argument for slavery with his assertion that "the slave is a slave by nature." This is consistent with a Greek and later European worldview that placed itself at the center of all rational thinking and reflection and all other races and cultures on the periphery. Aristotle's defense of dominance over people of different cultures and skin color provided a precedent for the justification of slavery and the apparent beginnings of racism in the West.[23] Therefore, for West, Greek aesthetic, cultural, and intellectual differences in comparison to peoples of African descent became the ideological basis for both African exclusion and domination by Greeks.

Enrique Dussel argues that Greeks justified their domination by distinguishing themselves from others using the philosophical categories of "Being" and "beings" wherein, "Being is; beings are what are seen and controlled." According to Dussel, this would serve as the defining characteristic of classic Greco-Roman philosophies:

> Classic Greco-Roman philosophies, with some exceptions, in fact articulated the interests of the dominant pro-slavery classes and justified their domination from the horizon of Being itself. It is easy to understand Aristotle's "The

[22] Ibid., 59.
[23] Joseph R. Washington, *The Politics of God* (Boston: Beacon Press, 1967) 8. While Washington recognizes the claims of Aristotelian scholars, particularly Ruth Benedict, that Aristotle had in mind cultural and not racial differences, he still maintains that the in-group/out-group schema lead to the emergence of racism on structural grounds. See ibid., 8ff.

slave is a slave by nature," or the inclination of Stoics and Epicureans to extend deliverance to all the citizens of the empire, so as to ensure a "good conscience" in all its members, on the one hand, and to sanctify the empire, finite manifestation of the gods of cosmopolitanism, on the other.[24]

Though the Mediterranean world would soon crumble, Europe would adopt its principles and "would begin to consider itself the archetypal foundational 'I.'" It would begin to articulate the interests of pro-slavery groups and to see "Being" as Europeans and "beings" as those of a lower order to be used and manipulated. According to Dussel:

> modern European philosophy, even before the *ego cogito*, but certainly from then on situated all men [sic] and all cultures—and with them their women and children—within its own boundaries as manipulable tools, instruments. Ontology understood them as interpretable beings, as known ideas, as mediations or internal possibilities within the horizon of the comprehension of Being.[25]

This reduction of other human beings to the status of manipulable tools and instruments by Europeans is seen most prominently in its treatment of Africans and, more importantly for our purposes, the intellectual justifications of it. Voltaire made his disdain for black humanity clear when he stated:

> The Negro is a species of [human] different from ours as the breed of spaniels is from that of greyhounds. The mucous membrane, or network, which nature has spread between the muscles and the skin, is white in us and black or copper-colored in them. . . .
>
> If their understanding is not of a different nature from ours, it is at least greatly inferior. They are not capable of any great application or association of ideas, and seemed formed neither for the advantages nor the abuses of philosophy.[26]

Inherent in Voltaire's statement is the European recognition of the aesthetic, cultural, and intellectual inferiority of blacks. This presupposition would guide the thinking of the most celebrated figures of the Western intellectual tradition.

David Hume, known more for his treatises on empiricism, played a major role in the development of pro-slavery literature. In his essay "Of National Characteristics" he wrote:

> I am apt to suspect the negroes, and in general all other species of men [sic] (for there are four or five different kinds) to be naturally inferior to the whites. There was never a civilized nation of any other complexion than

---

[24] Enrique Dussel, *Philosophy of Liberation* (Maryknoll, N.Y.: Orbis Books, 1990) 6.
[25] Ibid., 2–3.
[26] Taken from West, *Prophesy Deliverance!* 62.

white, nor even any individual eminent either in action or speculation. No ingenious manufactures amongst them, no arts, no sciences. . . .

   In Jamaica indeed they talk of one negroe as a man of parts and learning; but 'tis likely he is admired for very slender accomplishments, like a parrot, who speaks a few words plainly.[27]

Immanuel Kant, known more for his *Ding in sich,* clearly showed his loyalty to the Western intellectual tradition when he maintained that Africans "in virtue of their blackness, are precluded from the realm of reason and civilization."[28] For Kant, "so fundamental is the difference between the two races of men, and it appears to be as great in regard to mental capacities as in color."[29]

Hume's influence on Kant is expressed in Kant's *Observations on the Feeling of the Beautiful and Sublime* when he stated:

> Mr. Hume challenges anyone to cite a simple example in which a negro has shown talents, and asserts that among the hundreds of thousands of blacks who are transported elsewhere for their countries, although many of them have even been set free, still not a single one was ever found who presented anything great in art or science or any other praiseworthy quality, even though among the whites some continually rise aloft from the lowest rabble, and through superior gifts earn respect in the world.[30]

In regard to the intellectual capacity of blacks, Kant was convinced that blackness itself inhibited blacks from saying or thinking anything profound. According to Kant, "it might be that there was something in this which perhaps deserved to be considered; but in short, this fellow was quite black from head to foot, a clear proof that what he said was stupid."[31]

Hegel conceived of the German state as the existential manifestation of the absolute Idea, or God.[32] This meant the exclusion of those groups not of Germanic or European origin. The bigoted genius of Hegel was that he not only argued for the illegitimacy of black equality on aesthetic, cultural, and intellectual terms, but on nationalistic and continental terms as well. In his *Philosophy of History* Hegel asserts that Africa "is no historical part of the world; it has no movement or development to exhibit. Historical move-

---

[27] Taken from ibid. See also Richard H. Popkin, "Hume's Racism," *The Philosophical Forum* 9:2–3 (Winter–Spring 1977–1978); Richard H. Popkin, "The Philosophical Basis of Eighteenth-Century Racism," *Studies in Eighteenth-Century Culture* 3, ed. Harold E. Pagliano (Case Western Reserve University, 1973).

[28] Tsenay Serequeberhan, ed., *African Philosophy: The Essential Readings* (New York: Paragon House, 1991) 5.

[29] Taken from ibid., 5–6.

[30] Taken from West, *Prophesy Deliverance!* 62.

[31] Taken from ibid., 63.

[32] Taken from Serequeberhan, *African Philosophy,* 6.

ments in it—that is in its northern part—belong to the Asiatic or European World."[33]

In the *Philosophy of Right,* Hegel continues his anti-black perspective but understands it not to be racism but "the unfolding of Reason in its world-historical process of self-institution." "What the 'explorer' and the 'colonizer' express as a crude Eurocentric racism, Hegel and modern European philosophy articulate as the universality of Reason, the trademark of Europe. In fact, for Hegel, the possibility of 'ethical life' in the context of modernity is predicated on the necessity of colonial expansion."[34]

Marx would echo Hegel's sentiments regarding the necessity of colonial expansion. Though Marx saw the violent overthrow of the bourgeois by the proletariat as necessary for realizing the classless society, he also saw colonialism and its concomitant conditions as necessary to inspire the proletariat to revolution. Thus, the Marxist critique of idealist philosophy and European capitalism sees the possibility of the actualization of its critical project as directly linked to the colonial globalization of Europe.[35] The colonial Europeanization of the globe was a prerequisite for the possibility of true human freedom, that is, communism.[36] In plain terms, this means that the realization of the Marxist project (Communism) is based on the dehumanization and colonization of non-European peoples and races. Regarding England's role in European colonialist expansion, Marx wrote: "England has to fulfill a double mission in India; one destructive, the other regenerating—the annihilation of old Asiatic [African] society, and the laying of the material foundations of Western society in Asia [Africa]."[37] Thus, what seems to be a revolutionary philosophy on the surface was ultimately just as repressive as other European philosophies.

While there are slight variations philosophically concerning the above-mentioned thinkers, one constant remains: European humanity is the center of all meaningful philosophical reflection and cultural expression. But more important (especially in Hegel's case with the state being seen as the existential manifestation of absolute Spirit or God) is the thinking that the European mind and the mind of God are one.

> It is important to note that, behind and beyond the differing Eurocentric views of the above thinkers—and the modern tradition of Western philosophy as a whole—lies the *singular* and grounding metaphysical belief that European humanity is properly speaking isomorphic with the humanity of the

[33] Ibid.
[34] Taken from ibid.
[35] See Karl Marx and Frederick Engels, *On Colonialism* (New York: International Publishers, 1972; written in 1853).
[36] Ibid.
[37] Ibid.

human *as such*. Beyond all differences and disputes, this is the common thread that constitutes the unity of the tradition. Thus, European cultural-historical prejudgements are passed off as transcendental wisdom![38]

In other words, European philosophers saw their views as not only being existentially sound but metaphysically sound in that they understood the products of their minds and the mind of God to be inseparable.

This represents a cursory examination of the Western intellectual tradition in general. Let us now examine the Western theological tradition in particular through the lens of James Cone.

The Western Theological Tradition and Sociopolitical Oppression

Inasmuch as the Western theological tradition is but a microcosm of the Western intellectual tradition, it too has a history mired in sociopolitical oppression. Cone is particularly critical of the Western theological tradition insofar as it has consistently identified itself with the status quo and in so doing has been inconsistent with the gospel of Jesus Christ. Christian theologians, for Cone, have historically done theology based on Greek philosophy and the cultural and political values of white racism rather than on the biblical theme of God as the liberator of the oppressed. Cone puts it more succinctly:

> In the history of Western theology, we seldom find an ethic of liberation derived from the God of freedom, but rather, an ethic of the status quo, derived from Greek philosophy and from the political interests of a church receiving special favors from the state. Sometimes this status quo was expressed in terms of a philosophical emphasis on reason. At other times, the theme was faith, understood either as assent to propositional truths or as a spiritual relationship with God. Whatever the variation of emphases on faith and reason, God's revelation was interpreted, more often than not, as consistent with the values of the structures of political oppression.[39]

Thus, for Cone, despite the various ways in which revelation was treated in the Western theological tradition, they possessed one commonality: protecting the interests of privileged classes.

While Cone is somewhat concerned with the categories of Western theology, such as faith and reason, faith and history, the historical-critical method, etc., he is more concerned with their content being void of any reference to sociopolitical liberation as a basis of theologizing. In short, for Cone, the Western theological tradition's failure was and is its inability to transcend its limited, political interests that have been historically repressive for black people.

---

[38] Serequeberhan, *African Philosophy,* 7.
[39] James H. Cone, *God of the Oppressed* (San Francisco: Harper & Row, 1975) 197.

It is not that the problem of faith and history is unimportant. Rather, its importance, as defined by white theologians, is limited to their social interests. Although oppressed blacks are interested in faith as they struggle in history, the shape of the faith-history problem in contemporary American theology did not arise from the social existence of black people. On the contrary, its character was shaped by those who, sharing the consciousness of the Enlightenment, failed to question the consequences of the so-called enlightened view as reflected in the colonization and slavery of that period.[40]

While Cone concedes the virtue of the Enlightenment challenge of *sapere aude* (dare to think for yourself), he also rightly points out that this challenge was directed exclusively to Western humanity. For black and red peoples in North America, the spirit of the Enlightenment was socially and politically demonic, becoming a pseudo-intellectual basis for their enslavement and extermination.[41]

Yet despite these historical atrocities by whites on blacks and Native Americans, for Cone, white theologians continue to theologize from a white perspective. According to Cone, white theologians "have rarely attempted to transcend the social interests of their group by seeking an analysis of the gospel in light of the consciousness of black people struggling for liberation. White theologians, because of their identity with the dominant power structure, are largely boxed within their own cultural history."[42] Because that cultural history, in Cone's view, is rooted in the exaltation of whiteness at the expense of black people, it was assumed by white intellectuals and religious leaders that black people had nothing significant to contribute to theological reflection.

For Cone, identifying with the status quo is not limited to the Enlightenment or American theology but is consistent, with rare exception, with the entire Western theological tradition. Cone cites Constantine's conservative stance following the Arian controversy and its effect on the Church's politics and theology as the origin of a historical trend that divorced theological reflection from sociopolitical oppression. That was why the early Church Fathers could ask about the Son's relation to the Father (God) and later the Holy Spirit's relation to both without connecting the question to the historical freedom of the oppressed.[43]

The divorcing of theological reflection from the liberation of the oppressed emerged, in large part, in Cone's judgment, as a result of theologians being products of privileged classes. Therefore, for Cone, their theological presuppositions emerged out of their social context—a context committed

---

[40] Ibid., 46.
[41] Ibid.
[42] Ibid., 47.
[43] Ibid., 197–8.

to the preservation of the status quo. Moreover, according to Cone, their understanding of the gospel was/is inextricably bound with an existential reality that blinded them to the glaring inconsistency between an oppressive social context and God's revelation in Jesus Christ. Since the Church and its bishops (during the age of Constantine and thereafter) were not slaves, it did not occur to them that God's revelation in Jesus Christ is identical with the presence of God's Spirit in the slave community in struggle for the liberation of humanity.[44] Thus, Cone sees as the failure of the early Church (and the Western theological tradition, in general) its equating the gospel with the perpetuation of the status quo.

> Thus whatever else Christian ethics might be, it can never be identified with the actions of people who conserve the status quo. This was the essential error of the early Church. By becoming the religion of the Roman state, replacing the public state sacrifices, Christianity became the opposite of what Christ intended.[45]

Cone also saw this status quo tendency in the theologies of Augustine and Aquinas. Though they differed on the role of faith and reason in theological discourse, they were both advocates of slavery and denounced any form of revolutionary struggle. For Augustine, slavery was a result of the sinfulness of the slaves. For Aquinas, slavery was a part of the natural order of creation. For Augustine, "slaves are to be subject to their masters," carrying out their duties "with a good-heart and a good-will."[46] For Aquinas, "the slave, in regard to his master, is an instrument. . . . Between a master and his slave there is a special right of domination."[47]

This trend would continue into the Reformation, for Cone, beginning with Luther's condemnation of the Peasant Revolt. It led Luther to say that "nothing can be more poisonous, hurtful, or devilish than a rebel."[48] Cone looks upon this precision of language with suspicion insofar as it legitimates a "law and order" mentality giving repressive governments unbridled authority in putting down the oppressed's strivings for freedom.

> Luther's concern for "law and order" in the midst of human oppression is seriously questioned by Black Theology. While it may be doubtful whether his doctrine of the relation between church and state prepared the way for Hitler's genocide of the Jews in Europe, it did little to prevent it. In fact, his condemnation of the Peasant Revolt sounds very much like white churchmen's [sic] condemnation of ghetto rebellions.[49]

[44] Ibid., 198.
[45] Ibid.
[46] Taken from ibid.
[47] Taken from ibid.
[48] Taken from ibid.
[49] James H. Cone, *A Black Theology of Liberation* (New York: Lippincott, 1970) 71.

Further, Black Theology finds white religionists' condemnations of black uprisings particularly hypocritical insofar as very seldom do these same white religionists equally condemn the violence done to black people by repressive governments that inspire black revolution.[50]

Cone sees Calvin and Wesley as following suit. Cone is suspicious of the easy identification of Calvinism with capitalism and slave trading as exemplified by Max Weber in his *Protestant Ethic and the Spirit of Capitalism.* While Cone concedes that Wesley condemned slavery, his perspective is still suspect insofar as the overall tenor of Wesley's works reflect a greater concern for individual souls than sociopolitical oppression.

Cone has little patience with the argument that these thinkers did not make the gospel relevant to the oppressed because of the historical limitations of their existence. Is it fair, goes the argument, to criticize those of the sixteenth century while standing in the twentieth? For Cone, this would be to presuppose that we are now able to see the fallacies in the theologies of these thinkers and, more importantly, that we would not find similar errors today. But, in Cone's view, such is not the case.

According to Cone, the modern period is also guilty of this status quo tendency. Its modus operandi, for Cone, is to conceive of racism as one societal problem among many others, thereby diminishing its significance in the society.

> White theologians and ethicists simply ignore black people by suggesting that the problem of racism and oppression is only one social expression of a larger ethical concern. This error in contemporary ethical discourse is no different from Luther's error. It is an ethics of the status quo, primarily derived from an identity with the cultural values of white oppressors rather than the biblical theme of God's liberation of the oppressed.[51]

Cone saw Reinhold Niebuhr and Paul Ramsey as prime examples. The former asserted that "we must not consider the Founding Fathers immoral just because they were slaveholders."[52] The latter says that "simple and not so simple injustice alone has never been a sufficient justification for revolutionary change."[53] Cone attributes this aversion to the theme of liberation to a theological blindness endemic to the Western tradition itself. Using Christian ethicists as the basis of his critique, Cone explains:

This is not to suggest that Luther had no place in his thought for resisting the state. Regarding the Peasant Revolt, Luther harshly condemned the princes for creating the atmosphere that led to its emergence.

[50] See Cone's article "Black Theology on Revolution, Violence and Reconciliation," *Union Seminary Quarterly Review* 31:1 (Fall 1975) 5–14.

[51] Cone, *God of the Oppressed,* 201.

[52] Ibid.

[53] Ibid.

This blindness of Christian ethicists is not merely a cultural accident. As with Luther and others in the Western theological tradition, it is due to a *theological* blindness. White ethicists take their cue from their fellow theologians: because white theologians have not interpreted God as the Liberator of the oppressed, it follows that white ethicists would not make liberation the central motif of ethical analysis.[54]

This necessitates, for Cone, a new way of doing theology that challenges both the limited and racist context of white theology and that departs from the culture of the oppressed.

Why a Black Theology?

The above treatment of the Western intellectual/theological tradition clearly shows that it has been inimical to the interests of oppressed people, in general, and black people in particular. Thus what is needed, for Cone, is a new way of doing theology that strips whiteness of its power and elevates blackness as a means of empowering black people to do what they deem necessary to bring about its freedom. Cone sees this as consistent with the divine activity of God as revealed in Jesus to set free those held captive by oppressive political structures. This means that there is "a need for a theology whose sole purpose is to emancipate the gospel from its 'whiteness' so that blacks may be capable of making an honest self-affirmation through Jesus Christ."[55] This establishes Cone's theology as being in the process of deideologizing a white supremacist theological methodology.

Black self-affirmation, for Cone, must depart from an unmasking of the religio-political ideologies that create in blacks a nihilistic self-image and that falsely characterizes white humanity as superior. According to Cone, religio-political ideologies represent a distortion of the real content of religion and, more importantly, stifle the divine movement of freedom in and among blacks.

> Black religion and black people can never become what they ought to be (a religion and a people unreservedly devoted to the emancipation of all blacks) as long as the content of religion is a distorted reflection of the religion of the enslaver. To be free means to be free to create new possibilities for existence.[56]

Thus, for Cone, exposing the ideological nature of white religion and its debilitating effects on the black self-image is essential to a theology of liberation.

Cone sees this approach as having its roots in both pre-Civil War black preachers (as opposed to post-Civil War black preachers who assumed a

[54] Ibid.
[55] James H. Cone, *Black Theology and Black Power,* Twentieth Anniversary Edition (San Francisco: Harper & Row, 1989) 32.
[56] Ibid., 130.

more accommodating posture) and the emergence of Black Power. The former saw an inextricable link between the preaching of the gospel and the engendering of a spirit of sociopolitical freedom (as opposed to a purely spiritual freedom) among black people. The latter affirms the power of black people to define the limits of their existence independent of white intrusion. Further, Cone sees a dialectical interrelationship between Black Power and black religion. Black Power's recognition of the religious nature of black people is indispensable for its efficacy. Black religion sees Black Power as the medium through which it relates the condition of black people to the message of Jesus Christ.

> Therefore, Black Theology seeks to make black religion a religion of Black Power. It does not attempt to destroy Christianity but endeavors to point to its blackness. The task of Black Theology is to make Christianity really Christian by moving black people with a spirit of black dignity and self-determination so they can become what the Creator intended.[57]

Put another way, the task of Black Theology is to seek a synthesis between pre-Civil War black religion and Black Power such that it creates a new Christian tradition that (1) makes the black condition in America its point of departure and (2) destroys the influence of white theology on black self-determination. In so doing, it unseats white males as paragons of normative thinking and undermines their ideological impact on both blacks and whites.

The primary task of Black Theology is to relate the oppressed condition of blacks to the biblical witness, showing that the revelation of God is inseparable from the liberation of the oppressed. Further, it is to establish the revelation of God as one that manifests itself in "moments of oppression" in both biblical and modern history. It is God taking on the condition of the oppressed, making the oppressed's struggle for liberation God's own. This, for Cone, is the distinctive characteristic of divine activity. Therefore, if the suffering of God is revealed in the suffering of the oppressed, then it follows that theology cannot achieve its Christian identity apart from a systematic and critical reflection upon the history and culture of the victims of oppression.[58]

Therein lies the reason, for Cone, as to why the influence of white theology must be destroyed. It lacks a true Christian identity not only because it has not struggled with the contradiction between faith in a God of freedom and black enslavement but that it also sanctioned that enslavement on the grounds that it was God-ordained, making it an ideology of the most virulent form. Thus the sociopolitical liberation of black people was, conveniently, seldom an issue emerging in the white theological consciousness.

[57] Ibid.
[58] James H. Cone, "Black Theology in American Religion," *Journal of the American Academy of Religion* 53:3 (December 1985) 770.

> As white theology is largely defined by its response to modern and post-modern societies of Europe and America, usually ignoring the contradictions of slavery and oppression in black life, black religious thought is the thinking of slaves and of marginalized blacks whose understanding of God was shaped by the contradictions that white theologians ignored and regarded as unworthy of serious theological reflection.[59]

Thus the fundamental flaw of white theology for Cone was/is its inability to raise the question of the relevance of Jesus Christ for oppressed peoples. As a result, for Cone white theology needs to be liberated from itself—it needs to be deideologized. Regarding both theology and ethics, Cone explains:

> Because White theology and ethics have not asked this question, we conclude that they need to be liberated; that is, freed from the bondage of Whiteness as defined by the variant manifestations of racism. Theology and ethics need to undergo a revolutionary transformation so that the meaning of Christ and his church can be defined in the light of the weak and helpless rather than according to the economic and political interests of oppressors.[60]

Thus, what is needed, in Cone's view, is a Black Theology that not only asks the question of Jesus Christ and sociopolitical oppression, but makes that question its point of departure.

Cone, however, is no romanticist. He understands that articulating a Black Theology in a society committed to racism is a dangerous venture. Since Cone recognizes that racism is endemic to all institutions in the society, including the Church, anyone who challenges it will invariably be perceived as both "anti-Christian" and "unpatriotic."

> It is dangerous because the true prophet of the gospel of God must become both "anti-Christian" and "unpatriotic." It is impossible to confront a racist society with the meaning of human existence grounded in commitment to the divine, without at the same time challenging the very existence of the national structure and all of its institutions, especially the established church. All national institutions represent the interests of the society as a whole. We live in a nation which is committed to the perpetuation of white supremacy, and it will try to exterminate all who fail to assist it in this ideal.[61]

---

[59] Ibid., 756. For a more detailed examination of the influence of social context in the shaping of one's thought, see Werner Stark, *The Sociology of Knowledge* (London: Routledge and Kegan Paul, 1958); Peter Berger and Thomas Luckmann, *The Social Construction of Reality: A Treatise in the Sociology of Knowledge* (New York: Doubleday, 1967); Peter Berger, *The Sacred Canopy: Elements of a Sociological Theory of Religion* (New York: Doubleday, 1967).

[60] James H. Cone, "Black Power, Black Theology and the Study of Theology and Ethics," *Theological Education* 6 (Spring 1970) 203.

[61] Cone, *A Black Theology of Liberation,* 107–8.

Black Theology not only refuses to assist in the perpetuation of white supremacy but openly works for its demise inasmuch as the exaltation of whiteness has historically meant the degradation of blackness. Black Theology proclaims the reality of the biblical God who is actively destroying everything that is against the manifestation of human dignity among black people.[62] More importantly, Black Theology affirms that the revelation of the biblical God as a liberator assures the black community that its struggle to eradicate whiteness is God's struggle as well.

This is to be contrasted with what Cone refers to as the idol white God that has historically convinced black people that its liberation is purely ethereal and to be content with their earthly lot. It is the white God, for Cone, who "will point to a heavenly bliss as a means of directing black people away from earthly rage. Freedom comes when we realize that it is against our interests, as a self-determining black community, to point out the 'good' elements in an oppressive structure. *There are no assets to slavery!*"[63] According to Cone, it is deleterious to the black liberation struggle for black people to express faith in an idol white God that validates the dehumanization of oppressed people. Therefore, Black Theology seeks to deideologize, that is, to continually expose both the ubiquitous nature of racism and the white God as an ideological construct designed to establish and perpetuate the superiority of the white race.

> Every segment in this society participates in black oppression. To accept the white God, to see good in the evil, is to lose sight of the goal of the revolution—the destruction of everything "masterly" in the society. "All or nothing" is the only possible attitude for the black community.[64]

Black Theology, then, does not compromise the goal of liberation for a semi-oppressive society. Inasmuch as liberation means the complete destruction of whiteness, accepting anything less would be a contradiction in terms.

Thus Black Theology is a theology of black liberation. It seeks to empower black people to determine what is in their best interests socially, economically, politically, and religiously, and to destroy everything in the society that is inimical to those interests—namely, ideologies of white supremacy.

> Liberation means that the oppressed must define the structure and scope of reality for themselves without taking their cues from the oppressors. If there is one brutal fact that the centuries of White oppression have taught black people, it is that white people are rendered incapable of making any valid

[62] Ibid., 108.
[63] Ibid., 110.
[64] Ibid.

judgement about human existence. The goal of Black Theology is the destruction of everything *white* so that black people can be liberated from alien gods.[65]

Thus, black liberation is inseparable not only from the destruction of whiteness but, more importantly, from disempowering white ideological assertions about black humanity, for they have always meant death and enslavement to the black community.

Having established the necessity of Black Theology, the question still remains, what does black liberation from white supremacy have to do with the gospel of Jesus Christ?

Black Theology as Christian Theology

The relationship of Black Theology to Christian theology is difficult to articulate given that Black Theology is rooted in the particularity of black existence in white America whereas Christian theology has historically been treated as a universal phenomenon. The difficulty of this task lies not only in the immensity of the subject but, more importantly, in the assumed discontinuity between Black consciousness and the gospel of Jesus Christ.[66]

The basis of this assumed discontinuity, for Cone, lies in the fact that the Western theological tradition has historically treated Christian faith with no interest in color. In Cone's view, however, inasmuch as God reveals Godself in Jesus Christ as a liberator of the weak and helpless and inasmuch as we live in a world where black people are enslaved, segregated, and discriminated against precisely because of their blackness, there can be no relevant treatment of Christian faith without departing from the problem of color. Cone sees white theologians' colorless theological treatments and appeals to universalism as an ideological ruse, keeping theology abstract and unrelated to human suffering. While Cone agrees that Christian theology has a universal dimension, he also contends

> that there is no universalism that is not particular. Indeed, their insistence upon the universal note of the gospel arises out of their own political and social interests. As long as they can be sure that the gospel is *for everybody,* ignoring that God liberated a *particular* people from Egypt, came in a *particular* man called Jesus, and for the *particular* purpose of liberating the oppressed, then they can continue their idle talk about theological abstractions, failing to recognize that such talk is not the gospel unless it is related to the concrete freedom of the little ones.[67]

[65] Ibid., 118.

[66] Cone, "Black Power, Black Theology and the Study of Theology and Ethics," 202.

[67] James H. Cone, "Black Theology and Ideology: A Response to My Respondents," *Union Seminary Quarterly Review* 31:1 (Fall 1975) 82–3.

Thus, the assumed discontinuity between Black consciousness and the gospel of Jesus Christ, for Cone, is more an ideology of the Western theological consciousness than the revelation of the God of the Bible. According to Cone, because God reveals Godself in "moments of oppression," liberating the weak and helpless from sociopolitical oppression, there is a *distinct continuity* between black liberation and the gospel of Jesus Christ. Cone, then, sees the task of Christian theology as illuminating this continuity by relating the history of the Bible, with emphasis on the Exodus narrative, to the history of black people in America communicating the faith of the black community that God will liberate black people just as God did the Israelites. White theology's inability to recognize this correlation, for Cone, reveals its ideological tendencies and therefore precludes it from being Christian theology.

> No white theologian has taken color as a point of departure for doing theology. Apparently, white religionists see no correlation between Jesus Christ and the slaveships, the insurrections, the auction block, and the Black ghetto. They have not asked about Harlem and Watts because presumably they attach no special significance to Black presence in America. That is why Black theology questions whether White theology is Christian in any sense.[68]

But therein lies precisely, for Cone, why Black Theology is Christian theology. Not only does Black Theology see a correlation between Jesus Christ and the slave ships, the insurrections, the auction block, and the black ghetto, it also maintains that there can be no relevant treatment of Christian theology in modern times that does not depart from the black experience in America. Therefore, according to Black Theology, since God reveals Godself through Jesus as a liberator of the oppressed making the oppressed condition God's own, and since that oppressed people in America is black people, the reality of God in America is found only in black history and culture. "My point is that God came, and continues to come, to those who are poor and helpless for the purpose of setting them free. And since the people of color are [God's] elected poor in America, any interpretation of God that ignores black oppression cannot be Christian theology."[69] This means that Cone sees Christian theology as an explication of God's revelatory work on behalf of oppressed peoples. Black Theology asserts that that oppressed people in America is black people. Therefore, Black Theology is Christian theology insofar as the latter cannot divorce the revelatory work of God from the oppression of black people.

This is not to suggest that Black Theology's departure from the black condition denies the absolute revelation of God. Rather, it affirms absolute revelation by making it inseparable from the black struggle for liberation.

[68] Cone, "Black Power, Black Theology and the Study of Theology and Ethics," 206.
[69] Cone, "Black Theology and Ideology," 83.

> Black Theology is Christian theology precisely because it has the black predicament as its point of departure. It calls upon black people to affirm God because [God] has affirmed us. [God's] affirmation is made known not only in [God's] election of oppressed Israel, but more especially in [God's] coming to us and being rejected in Christ for us. The event of Christ tells us that the oppressed blacks are [God's] people because, and only because, they represent who [God] is.[70]

Thus absolute revelation, for Cone, is universal, but because there is no universalism without being particular, any treatment of absolute revelation must root itself in a particular, concrete human condition, that is, the condition of the oppressed.[71]

According to Cone, since God reveals Godself to oppressed humanity, in general, and the black condition, in particular, blackness symbolically takes on a form of existential sacredness revealing God's stance in the black-white struggle. Black is holy, that is, it is a symbol of God's presence in history on behalf of the oppressed [humanity].[72] Further, since blackness is the symbolic locus of God's presence in history, for Cone, and since blackness represents human oppression, God in Christ takes on blackness, transforming the oppressed condition of blacks into a liberated one.

> Where there is black, there is oppression; but blacks can be assured that where there is blackness, there is Christ who has taken on blackness so that what is evil in [humanity's] eyes might become good. Therefore Christ is black because he is oppressed, and oppressed because he is black.[73]

This is why, in Cone's judgment, it is a theological impossibility to do Christian theology in the twentieth century and not see Christ as black. Just as Jesus was born as an oppressed Jew and dedicated his life to unmasking the religio-political ideologies in Palestine in the first century, so too is the spirit of Christ present among oppressed blacks in the twentieth century effectuating God's will among black people.

> Thinking of Christ as non-black in the twentieth century is as theologically impossible as thinking of him as non-Jewish in the first century. God's Word in Christ not only fulfills [God's] purposes for [humanity] through [God's] elected people, but also inaugurates a new age in which all oppressed people become [God's] people. In America, that people is a black people. In order to remain faithful to [God's] Word in Christ, [God's] present manifestation must be the very essence of blackness.[74]

---

[70] Cone, *Black Theology and Black Power,* 118.
[71] Ibid.
[72] Ibid., 69.
[73] Ibid.
[74] Ibid.

Thus the blackness of God means that God is making God's will known to black people that its strivings to unmask white theology and the Western intellectual tradition in general as ideologies that protect white national and global interests is synonymous with God's will.

Black Theology is Christian theology, for Cone, not only because God reveals Godself in the black condition, but also reveals Godself such that it affirms black peoples' strivings for liberation by whatever means the black community deems necessary. Further, Cone sees the biblical revelation of God as a liberator as confirming for black people that God did not ordain their enslavement and therefore that human salvation means not only being saved from "the bondage of sin and satan," but from the dehumanizing effects of white supremacy.

> Contemporary Black theology, taking its cue from black religionists of the past, believes that Christ, because he is the oppressed one whose resurrection binds him to all who are enslaved, must be inseparable from the humiliated condition of black people. By becoming as we are in our Blackness, we now know that we are not what the world says. The knowledge of Christ frees us to do what we must, knowing that our Blackness has been bought with the price of his death. We are saved: saved from the White way of life and its dehumanizing effects on the Black community, and saved into the Black way of life; i.e., the freedom to be what we are and do what we must so that Black liberation will become a reality in this land.[75]

Thus, Black Theology does not share white admonitions to "Let the Lord handle it" when it comes to black liberation. Rather, Black Theology claims that the knowledge of Christ frees black people to struggle for its and humanity's liberation knowing that the affirmation of blackness is the affirmation of salvation.

Finally, Cone's treatment of the cross and resurrection show God's revelation, from a particular standpoint, as that which guarantees the oppressed victory in its liberation struggle and, from a universal standpoint, frees all, regardless of color, who work for the liberation of the oppressed.

> The resurrection is the good news of the liberation victory. Jesus is not dead but is alive, because God's will to liberate the weak and helpless cannot be defeated. Indeed the resurrection is the divine disclosure that all of the oppressed peoples throughout the world can now share in God's liberation by fighting for the freedom of the poor in their own midst. The cross is the particularization of the election of the oppressed, and the resurrection is its universality, namely, the divine will to grant freedom to all who struggle for the liberation of the humiliated and abused.[76]

[75] Cone, "Black Power, Black Theology, and the Study of Theology and Ethics," 213.

[76] Cone, "Black Theology and Ideology," 84–5.

Thus, Cone recognizes the universality of the gospel but maintains that it must manifest itself in the participation of the oppressed struggle for liberation. Any other treatment of universalism, for Cone, is a betrayal of the gospel.

Conclusion

We began the chapter by showing that both the Western intellectual tradition in general and the Western theological tradition in particular have historically been pro-slavery and anti-black. We then examined the theology of Cone showing how he (1) applied his ideological suspicion to the Western intellectual/theological tradition in exposing it as part of an ideological superstructure that seeks to legitimate white supremacy; (2) developed new theological presuppositions as a means of empowering black people to challenge white supremacy; and (3) equated those presuppositions with the revelation of God in Jesus Christ, thereby "debunking" the Western tradition's assumption that there is a discontinuity between Black consciousness and the gospel of Jesus Christ. Since Cone was able to recognize the ideological tendencies of the Western intellectual/theological tradition, to see it as a medium for protecting the social, economic, and political interests of the white community, and, more importantly, to recognize that relevant theological reflection must seek to destroy the credibility of it, he passes the second stage of Segundo's hermeneutic circle.

CHAPTER 3

Hermeneutical Methodology and the Emergence of Exegetical Suspicion

The third stage of the hermeneutic circle requires that we experience a new theological reality, given by the previous stages, such that it leads us to an exegetical suspicion or "the suspicion that the prevailing interpretation of the Bible has not taken important pieces of data into account." This means, for Segundo, a new way of doing theology with an "act of will,"[1] such that it roots theological reflection in the service of an oppressed community struggling for liberation and takes it out of the community of oppressors who use theology as a vehicle to justify that oppression. For the purposes of this chapter, it means an examination of the ideology of the biblical legitimacy of black oppression. It also means an examination of the hermeneutical methodology of Black Theology that exposes the ideological nature of the biblical defense of the enslavement and segregation of black people and creates new presuppositions that effectively counter it. Thus, the new direction to be taken by scriptural interpretation will be dictated by the uncovering of the mechanisms of ideology and by the will to root them out of theology.[2] Therefore, I proceed to show that Cone passes the third stage of the hermeneutic circle in the following way. First, I examine the hermeneutical methodology of the ideology of white supremacy during American slavery, looking at both Old and New Testaments. Second, I analyze the hermeneutical methodology of white supremacy during segregation, showing how the same presuppositions used during slavery were adapted by segregationists

---

[1] See Karl Mannheim, *Ideology and Utopia: An Introduction to the Sociology of Knowledge* (New York: Harcourt, Brace and World, 1966). For Segundo's treatment of it see *The Liberation of Theology,* trans. John Drury (Maryknoll, N.Y.: Orbis Books, 1976) 8ff.

[2] Segundo, *The Liberation of Theology,* 29. By "hermeneutic methodology" I mean a methodological way of interpreting the Bible such that it clearly sets forth what the thinker considers to be the central theme of Scripture. As such, my understanding of hermeneutical methodology is closely akin to what is commonly referred to as "biblical hermeneutics."

to justify racial segregation. I then move into the theology of Cone, elaborating on the hermeneutical methodology of Black Theology from both Old and New Testament perspectives showing how it deideologizes the ideological/methodological claims of slaveholders and segregationists.

Hermeneutical Methodology, White Supremacy, and Slavery

According to James O. Buswell, in his book *Slavery, Segregation, and Scripture,* scriptural justifications of slavery took on several forms, either as one argument or a combination of arguments. These arguments can be divided into four groups: (1) general assertions that the institution was natural, "ordained of God," and of benefit to the enslaved; (2) examples of slavery described or alluded to in the Bible, chiefly in the Old Testament; (3) instructions regarding behavior of slaves and masters, chiefly in the New Testament; and (4) underlying the whole structure of the defense system (and constituting the major basis for the scriptural defense of racial segregation since post-Emancipation times), the supposed teachings regarding the black race, chiefly based upon elaborations on the story of Ham and the curse of Noah.[3]

Though there was constant disagreement in the slaveholding community regarding the christianization of the slave, there was general agreement that slavery was God-ordained and beneficial to the enslaved. From the very origins of the African slave trade, white slaveholders saw slavery as a divinely appointed institution erected by God for the purposes of civilizing "heathen Africans." Not only was the institution of slavery given Divine sanction, but the slave trade itself and the entire destiny of heathen Africans being brought to America was considered "legal," "licit," "in accordance with humane principles and the laws of revealed religion," and "a merciful visitation," on the grounds that it was the means of their hearing the gospel.[4] Further, slavery (as opposed to missionaries) was seen by many whites as the most effective medium for christianizing blacks. According to *The Southern Literary Messenger* of January 1835, slavery

> has done more to elevate a degraded race in the scale of humanity, to tame the savage, to civilize the barbarous, to soften the ferocious, to enlighten the ignorant, and to spread the blessings of Christianity among the heathen than all the missionaries that philanthropy and religion have ever sent forth.[5]

Whether the intent was to civilize or christianize, slavery was seen as an indispensable medium for their realization. Slaveholders fundamentally held

---

[3] James O. Buswell III, *Slavery, Segregation, and Scripture* (Grand Rapids, Mich.: Eerdmans, 1964) 12.

[4] Ibid., 13–14.

[5] Quoted in ibid., 14.

that "to expect to civilize or Christianize the negro without the intervention of slavery is to expect an impossibility."[6] This philosophy would hold true even for famous evangelist George Whitfield who in 1751 wrote that,

> though liberty is a sweet thing to such as are born free, yet those who may never know the sweets of it, slavery perhaps may not be so irksome. I should think myself highly favored if I could purchase a good number of them, in order to make their lives comfortable, and lay a foundation for breeding up their posterity in the nurture and admonition of the Lord.[7]

Thus, for Whitfield, to speak of freedom for those born into slavery is to ignore the anthropological nature of the slave and, more importantly, precludes slaveholders from carrying out their divine duty to christianize slaves.

Pro-slavery advocates cited the biblical revelations that Abraham, Isaac, and Jacob owned slaves as God's affirmation of slavery. But what would serve as the two most prominent narratives of the pro-slavery argument were Leviticus 25:44-46 (Hebrew instructions regarding slaves) and Genesis 9:18-27 (the curse on Ham). Of particular significance for slaveholders concerning the Leviticus narrative was, "It is from the nations around you that you may acquire male and female slaves. . . . You may keep them as a possession for your children after you, for them to inherit as property." This proved for slave masters that God extended to the Hebrews, "a written permit . . . to *buy, hold, and bequeath, men and women,* to perpetual servitude."[8] Thus, owning slaves was seen as a theistic command and not a human freedom. Slaveholders cited the fact that the authorized (King James) version used the word "shall" rather than "may" as proof that "God *commanded* them [Israelites] to be slaveholders. [God] *made it* the law of their social state."

However, this left pro-slavery advocates with another issue regarding slavery's eternal nature. Did God intend for slavery to continue into eternity or only until the ceremonial rites of the Hebrews were abolished? This question would be taken up most notably by James Smylie. He argued that although certain ceremonial laws were to be observed for a limited period of time, the Decalogue was eternal insofar as it was "engraven, not written, on two tables of stone," "engraven" meaning that God wrote the Decalogue, thereby making slavery God's will eternally. Therefore, for Smylie, since both

---

[6] Ibid.

[7] Ibid. See W. S. Jenkins, *Pro-Slavery Thought in the Old South* (Chapel Hill: University of North Carolina Press, 1935) 42.

[8] Quoted in H. Shelton Smith, *In His Image, but . . . Racism in Southern Religion: 1780–1910* (Durham, N.C.: Duke University Press, 1972) 132. See Thornton Stringfellow, *A Brief Examination of Scripture Testimony on the Institution of Slavery* (Richmond: n.p., 1841); see also Albert T. Bledsoe, *An Essay on Liberty and Slavery* (Philadelphia: Lippincott, 1856).

the fourth[9] and tenth[10] commandments concern human bondage, God meant for it to extend beyond ceremonial laws. Establishing slavery's eternal nature was crucial for pro-slavery advocates inasmuch as it would serve as the link that connected biblical slavery to modern slavery. If God foresaw or intended that servitude should expire with the Mosaic ritual, the authority of masters probably would not be recognized in a law intended to be perpetual; nor would there have been, as is the fact, a recognition made of servants as property.[11]

By far, the most widely used scriptural justification of black enslavement was the curse on Ham or the Hamitic hypothesis (Gen 9:18-27). It holds that Noah was mocked in his nakedness by son Ham and, when made aware of it, Noah sentenced Ham and his posterity to be slaves eternally to brothers Shem and Japheth and their posterity. Most importantly, it was believed that Ham was of African descent while Shem and Japheth were of European descent, thus biblically affirming the enslavement of Africans by Europeans. Since Ham was considered to be the father of Canaan, Noah proclaimed: "Cursed be Canaan; / lowest of slaves shall he be to his brothers" (v. 25). Thus, the Hamitic defense of slavery rested on the rather spurious assumption that all Africans were descendants of Canaan and that Jews and Gentiles were the progeny of Shem and Japheth.[12]

According to H. Shelton Smith, this text served two purposes. First, it affirmed for slaveholders that slavery was a product of the mind of God and not humans. Though Smith rightly points out that Noah was still inebriated and enraged about Ham's mockery, it did not prevent a prominent Methodist minister from saying that "he spoke under the impulse and dictation of Heaven." With that being the case, slaveholders saw Noah as the medium through which God spoke not only in ordaining slavery but in confirming its eternal nature. "His words were the words of God [Godself], and by them was slavery ordained. This was an early arrangement of the Almighty, to be perpetuated through all time."[13] The second purpose of the Hamitic

---

[9] Exod 20:8-10: "Remember the sabbath day, and keep it holy. Six days you shall labor and do all your work. But the seventh day is a sabbath to the LORD your God; you shall not do any work—you, your son or your daughter, your male or female slave, your livestock, or the alien resident in your towns."

[10] Exod 20:17: "You shall not covet your neighbor's house; you shall not covet your neighbor's wife, or male or female slave, or ox, or donkey, or anything that belongs to your neighbor."

[11] Quoted in Smith, *In His Image, but,* 132.

[12] James H. Evans, Jr., *We Have Been Believers: An African-American Systematic Theology* (Minneapolis: Fortress Press, 1992) 36.

[13] Quoted in Smith, *In His Image, but,* 130. See Alexander McCaine, *Slavery Defended from Scripture, Against the Attacks of the Abolitionists, in a Speech Delivered Before the General Conference of the Methodist Protestant Church, in Baltimore, 1842*

hypothesis was that it allegedly established blacks as slaves and whites as slaveholders. According to a South Carolina preacher and slaveholder:

> It is generally believed that Africans or Negroes, are the descendants of Ham; and it is by no means improbable that the very name Ham, which signifies burnt or black, was given to him prophetically, on account of the countries that his posterity were destined to inhabit. The judicial curse of Noah upon the posterity of Ham, seems yet to rest upon them.[14]

Further proof of the biblical affirmation of black servitude was Ham's supposed marrying into the race of Cain who had been cursed with a black skin for murdering brother Abel. This was a clear confirmation for pro-slavery devotees that all of Ham's descendants, not just those of Canaan, were Africans and therefore destined to be slaves eternally. This view was put forth by John Fletcher of Louisiana, originally a northerner who became one of the South's most vigilant pro-slavery ideologues.

> In his view, Ham's sin—and the sin denoted in the judicial curse—was racial amalgamation. The wayward son had contaminated his own race by marrying into the race of Cain, who in consequence of having slain his brother Abel had been smitten with a black skin. On this account, all of Ham's descendants, and not merely those of Canaan, were Africans or Negroes. On the other hand, Shem and Japheth were blessed with white descendants because they had married within their own race. It was only right therefore that the degenerate black descendants of Ham were doomed to perpetual servitude to the superior white offspring of Shem and Japheth.[15]

This solidified for slaveholders that there was a divine continuity of black enslavement from biblical to modern history and that its nature was eternal.

According to James Evans, the Hamitic hypothesis not only provided a defense of black enslavement, but was instrumental in providing a justification for the entire Southern way of life and therefore the South's self-perception.

> Thus the Ham story provided more than merely a defense for the repugnant institution of chattel slavery. It also rendered justification for an emerging

---

(Baltimore: n.p., 1842) 5; Frederick Dalcho, *Practical Considerations Founded on the Scriptures, Relative to the Slave Population of South Carolina* (Charleston, S.C.: n.p., 1823) 8–18; Patrick H. Mell, *Slavery: A Treatise Showing that Slavery Is Neither a Moral, Political, nor Social Evil* (Penfield, Ga.: n.p., 1844) 15.

[14] Quoted in Smith, *In His Image, but,* 130–1. For more elaborate accounts see Samuel Dunwoody, "A Sermon Upon the Subject of Slavery" (Columbia, S.C.: n.p., 1837); see also James A. Sloan, "The Great Question Answered, or Is Slavery a Sin in Itself?" (Memphis: n.p., 1857).

[15] Quoted in Smith, *In His Image, but,* 131. See Fletcher, *Studies on Slavery, in Easy Lessons* (Natchez, Miss.: n.p., 1852) 435–77; see also Nathan Lord, *A Letter of Inquiry to Ministers of the Gospel of All Denominations on Slavery* (Hanover, N.H.: n.p., 1860) 5–6.

Southern culture and an ascendent Southern economy, as well as explaining how humanity could, given a common ancestor in Noah, find itself divided into two classes of beings, subhuman slaves and superhuman masters.[16]

Thus, what was at stake for Southerners was the defense of a cultural expression whose cogency rested on establishing God's favor with the white race while holding another race in bondage.

In regard to the New Testament, pro-slavery ideologues centered their arguments around nine passages in five categories. They were: (1) obedience and subservience of the slave (Titus 2:9-10; Eph 6:5-9; Col 3:22-25; and 1 Pet 2:18-25);[17] (2) regard for the master (1 Tim 6:1-2; Eph 6:5-9);[18] (3) that one

---

[16] Evans, *We Have Been Believers*, 36. See Evans' recognition of Charles Copher's insight that after 1800 a "new Hamitic hypothesis" emerged that sought to remove black people from the Bible altogether by arguing that the blacks of the Bible were "Caucasoid Blacks." The corollary of this assertion is that Africans are not only not a part of biblical history, but are viewed as being incapable of civilization. It is my purpose only to show that the Hamitic hypothesis, in whatever form, played a major role in the hermeneutical methodology of white supremacy.

[17] Titus 2:9-10: "Tell slaves to be submissive to their masters and to give satisfaction in every respect; they are not to talk back, not to pilfer, but to show complete and perfect fidelity, so that in everything they may be an ornament to the doctrine of God our Savior."

Eph 6:5-9: "Slaves, obey your earthly masters with fear and trembling, in singleness of heart, as you obey Christ; not only while being watched, and in order to please them, but as slaves of Christ, doing the will of God from the heart. Render service with enthusiasm, as to the Lord and not to men and women, knowing that whatever good we do, we will receive the same again from the Lord, whether we are slaves or free.

"And masters, do the same to them. Stop threatening them, for you know that both of you have the same Master in heaven, and with [God] there is no partiality."

Col 3:22-25: "Slaves, obey your earthly masters in everything, not only while being watched and in order to please them, but wholeheartedly, fearing the Lord. Whatever your task, put yourselves into it, as done for the Lord and not for your masters, since you know that from the Lord you will receive the inheritance as your reward; you serve the Lord Christ. For the wrongdoer will be paid back for whatever wrong has been done, and there is no partiality."

1 Pet 2:18-21: "Slaves, accept the authority of your masters with all deference, not only those who are kind and gentle but also those who are harsh. For it is a credit to you if, being aware of God, you endure pain while suffering unjustly. If you endure when you are beaten for doing wrong, what credit is that? But if you endure when you do right and suffer for it, you have God's approval. For to this you have been called, because Christ also suffered for you, leaving you an example, so that you should follow in his steps."

[18] 1 Tim 6:1-2: "Let all who are under the yoke of slavery regard their masters as worthy of all honor, so that the name of God and the teaching may not be blas-

should remain in a state of calling (1 Cor 7:20-24);[19] (4) that a runaway should be returned (Philemon);[20] and (5) that God intended variety in human status (1 Cor 12:13-26).[21]

While the Old Testament provided the biblical rationale for slavery from a structural standpoint, the New Testament provided the ethical directives for the master-slave relationship. Although pro-slavery advocates acknowledged that there were no explicit passages in the New Testament that sanctioned involuntary servitude, they also contended that there were none that abrogated it. Thus, for the pro-slavery community, the New Testament was seen as an ethical guide seeking the fulfillment of what the Old Testament commanded. Put more simply, for pro-slavery advocates, the Old Testament was seen as authoritative in the Christian era unless it was nullified by the New Testament. This was the position of Richard Fuller, a prominent South Carolina Baptist clergyman and leading pro-slavery proponent. While in dialogue with Francis Wayland, a fellow pro-slavery advocate and president of Brown University, Fuller stated, "What God sanctioned in the Old Testament and permitted in the New, cannot be sin."[22] Further, Fuller "considered slavery to be permitted if it was nowhere explicitly condemned in the New Testament. That is to say, silence was tantamount to sanction."[23] An example

---

phemed. Those who have believing masters must not be disrespectful to them on the ground that they are members of the church; rather they must serve them all the more, since those who benefit by their service are believers and beloved."

[19] 1 Cor 7:20-24: "Let each of you remain in the condition in which you were called.

"Were you a slave when called? Do not be concerned about it. Even if you can gain your freedom, make use of your present condition now more than ever. For whoever was called in the Lord as a slave is a freed person belonging to the Lord, just as who was free when called is a slave of Christ. You were bought with a price; do not become slaves of human masters. In whatever condition you were called, brothers and sisters, there remain with God."

[20] The reader is encouraged to read the entire book of Philemon. Paul urges runaway slave Onesimus to return to his owner, Philemon. Though short in length (25 verses), its impact was huge in pro-slavery hermeneutical methodology.

[21] 1 Cor 12:22-25: "On the contrary, the members of the body that seem to be weaker are indispensable, and those members of the body that we think less honorable we clothe with greater honor, and our less respectable members are treated with greater respect; whereas our more respectable members do not need this. But God has so arranged the body, giving the greater honor to the inferior member, that there may be no dissension within the body, but the members may have the same care for one another."

[22] Quoted in Smith, *In His Image, but,* 133. See *Domestic Slavery Considered as a Scriptural Institution: In a Correspondence Between Rev. Richard Fuller of Beaufort, S.C., and the Rev. Francis Wayland, of Providence, R.I.* (New York: n.p., 1845) 170.

[23] Smith, *In His Image, but,* 133.

of "the silence-sanction" argument for pro-slavery proponents was that Jesus never condemned or alluded to the institution of slavery. Therefore, reasoned pro-slavery advocates, it must not be contrary to the will of God. This lead the slaveholding community theologically to assert that the Christ-event fulfills the patriarchal tradition rather than abrogating it. This view treats Jesus "as the continuation of the work of God in Israel, and therefore the fulfillment of the patriarchal tradition rather than the destroyer of it. In other words, any new dispensation by Jesus was not incompatible with the Old Law."[24] For pro-slavery ideologues, Jesus established *no new principles* but simply restated the Old Testament social arrangement for his own era.[25]

According to Bishop John England of the Diocese of Charleston, "the fact that Jesus in his parables made pedagogical use of the master-slave relation (as in Luke 17:7-10) without ever condemning slavery signified that he did not regard it as sinful in principle."[26] James Smylie argued that if the relation of master and slave had been inherently sinful, Jesus would have been sure to make that fact clear when he healed the sick bondsman of the centurion (Luke 7:2-10).[27] However, Smylie points out, Jesus not only did not reprimand the centurion for being a slaveholder, he told the centurion that his faith was the greatest in all Israel. From Smylie's standpoint, "His High approbation of the Centurion was certainly calculated to leave the impression that slaveholding and Christianity were not inconsistent with each other."[28] A similar argument put forth is that if Jesus had considered slavery to be a moral evil, he would not have failed to denounce it when preaching to Jewish congregations in which there were slaveholders.[29]

The epistles of Paul proved an even more amenable source for pro-slavery ideology. They contained specific instructions on the duties of masters and slaves. In fact, virtually every pro-slavery tract of any consequence explored the Pauline epistles far more exhaustively than any other portion of the New Testament.[30] For H. Shelton Smith, this was so for two reasons. First, Paul spoke only of duties of slaves and masters as if slavery was a given in human relationships. For slaveholders this meant, at the very least, implicit approval of slavery as an institution.

> Had Paul perceived the slightest moral taint in human bondage, he never would have been content merely to advise masters to treat their slaves justly

---

[24] Evans, *We Have Been Believers,* 38.
[25] Ibid. See Stringfellow, *A Brief Examination of Scripture,* 155.
[26] Smith, *In His Image, but,* 133.
[27] Ibid.
[28] Ibid.
[29] Ibid., 133–4.
[30] Ibid., 134.

and fairly; he would certainly have warned them to let the oppressed go free. Besides, if he had really felt that slaveholding was a sin, Paul would not have returned his newly won convert, Onesimus, to his owner, Philemon, without making this fact absolutely clear.[31]

Indeed, the key New Testament text for slaveholders was Paul's letter to Philemon. Slaveholders saw it as "the Pauline mandate" for slavery.

Second, pro-slavery advocates cited the fact that, in biblical history, slaveholders were members of churches founded by Paul. For slaveholders in the South this "demonstrated that the early church did not consider slaveholding sinful per se. They were the more certain of this, because applicants for admission to the primitive churches and to the sacraments were subjected to the most rigorous examination with respect to their spiritual qualifications for these privileges."[32] Thus, slaveholders saw the "conspicuous omission" of slaveholding as being sinful to the apostles as the central thesis of their treatment of the New Testament. According to Fuller:

> Before Baptism, [the apostles] required [humans] to repent, that is, to abandon all their sins; yet they baptized masters holding slaves. They fenced the Lord's table with the most solemn warnings . . . that to eat and drink unworthily was to eat and drink condemnation; yet they admitted to the table masters holding slaves.[33]

This solidified, for slaveholders, that Christianity and slavery were not inconsistent.

Let us now examine the hermeneutical methodology of white supremacy during segregation, seeing how its presuppositions differed, if at all, from those of slavery.

Hermeneutical Methodology, White Supremacy, and Segregation

The arguments in support of racial segregation emerge from the same four categories as those of slavery. They are: (1) segregation is of divine origin, of benefit to blacks and a part of the natural order; (2) examples of segregation in the Old Testament; (3) examples of segregation in the New Testament; and (4) teachings regarding the black race.[34]

Supporters of racial segregation, both in the North and South, are certain that it is a "law of God," "the plan and purpose of God," and "in accord with the Divine Will of God as manifested in the Created Order."[35]

---

[31] Ibid., 135.

[32] Ibid.

[33] Ibid., 135–6.

[34] Buswell, *Slavery, Segregation, and Scripture*, 55.

[35] Quoted in ibid. See also Tom Brady, "Segregation and the South," *Baptist Bulletin* (1951) 15; Kenneth Kinney, "The Segregation Issue," *Baptist Bulletin* (1956) 8; James P. Dees, "A Survey of the Racial Issue," *The Defender* (November 1958) 28–33.

Further, assertions that segregation has been of benefit to blacks were numerous and are reflected in the statement of clergyman G. T. Gillespie in an address to the Mississippi Synod of the Presbyterian Church:

> The southern negro has somehow managed to acquire a great number of homes, farms, banks, and other properties, has achieved a higher standard of living and today enjoys larger educational and economic opportunities, is happier and better adjusted, than can be said of any comparable number of his race at any time in their history or in any part of the world today.[36]

Thus, segregation was seen by many white clergymen as not only ordained of God but the only system that has the ability to significantly advance the lot of blacks. This is why segregationists consistently used the term "Southern negro" in arguing that the plight of southern blacks was comparable to that of blacks anywhere else in the world and that segregation was the reason for it. For Buswell, however, this represents a contradiction in terms insofar as it, on the one hand, points out the progress of blacks in a system of segregation while, on the other, depicts blacks in negative terms that are ontological in nature. It seems never to be realized that in many cases the same author who takes such pains in pointing out the progress of blacks under segregation, takes equal pains to paint a dark picture of their diseases, their immorality, their shiftlessness, and their stupidity.[37] Put more succinctly, for Buswell,

> It seems never to have dawned on white segregationists that when such inferiorities are attributed to race and offered as reasons to perpetuate the system, the Negroes continue to be treated in such a way as to actually increase the symptoms which are thought to make segregation necessary in the first place![38]

As for the Old Testament, segregationists primarily employed two passages: the curse on Ham (Genesis 9) and the Tower of Babel (Genesis 11). Segregationists argued that the Hamitic hypothesis was God's way of inaugurating the segregation of Noah's three sons. Further, this was also God's way of assigning an inferior status to those of African descent by selecting Ham as the son who mocked his father Noah. This, in turn, means that the sons of Shem and Japheth (European in descent) are appointed a superior status and commanded by order of divine right to rule over the children of Ham. Gillespie puts it this way:

---

[36] Buswell, *Slavery, Segregation, and Scripture,* 56. Taken from G. T. Gillespie, "A Christian View of Segregation" (Greenwood, Miss.: Citizens' Council Educational Fund, 1954) 7.

[37] Buswell, *Slavery, Segregation, and Scripture,* 56.

[38] Ibid.

> Since for two thousand years the practice of segregation was imposed upon
> the Hebrew people by Divine authority and express command, and infrac-
> tions of the command were punished with extreme severity, there is certainly
> no ground for the charge that racial segregation is displeasing to God, unjust
> to [humans], or inherently wrong.[39]

Such a position is highly untenable given that, although it is an inference
drawn from scripture, it ultimately possesses no solid scriptural foundation.
For instance, Gillespie fails to consider other human characteristics in the
Bible upon which separation occurred, nor does he consider, or may not
even be aware, that the populations were of the same race at the time the
narrative was written. Thus, it begs the question as to how one biblically justifies the segregation of humans on the basis of race and, if one does, what
is to be said about the segregation of humans on the basis of other human
characteristics.

The remaining Old Testament narrative used by segregationists was the
Tower of Babel. Its significance to segregationists was that it was used to
show God's disdain with integration. For segregationists, the confusion of
languages at Babel "indicates that the development of different languages
was not merely natural or accidental, but served as a Divine purpose, in becoming one of the most effective means of preserving the separate existence
of the general racial groups."[40]

This argument, however, stands on less plausible grounds than the
curse on Ham. Given that the narrative speaks of a confusion of tongues, it
nowhere suggests that the separation occurred on the basis of race. More
importantly, if the races are to be scattered to different geographical loca-
tions, as segregationists argue, that would not only preclude blacks and
whites from living in the same geographical area but also the right of whites
to enslave and segregate blacks.

The New Testament basis for segregation centered around the nine passages used in slavery as well as Acts 17:26. Though the first part of verse 26
refers to God having made of one blood all races, segregationists lifted up
the second half of verse 26, "having determined allotted periods and the
boundaries of their habitation." Thus, the argument follows from segregationists that God allotted this period and these boundaries for blacks to be
segregated by whites. This passage is then connected by segregationists with
the progeny of Noah's sons.

This statement of Gillespie concerning Christ and the apostles sums up
the New Testament segregationist view:

> Since Christ and the Apostles taught the love of God for all [humankind],
> the oneness of believers in Christ, and demonstrated that the principles of

[39] Taken from ibid., 58.
[40] Taken from ibid., 59.

Christian [personhood] and charity could be made operative in all relations of life, without demanding revolutionary changes in the natural or social order, there would appear to be no reason for concluding that segregation is in conflict with the spirit and teachings of Christ and the apostles and therefore un-Christian.[41]

Thus, for segregationists, the love of God for all humans does not suggest, as abolitionists argue, a change in the "lots" of races. Rather, it would be a violation of God's divinely created order to seek revolutionary changes in society. Such a change, for segregationists, would in fact be desegregation or, more appropriately, integration.

Having examined the hermeneutical methodology of white supremacy, that is, those biblical passages used in defense of African slavery, let us now take a look at the response of Black Theology.

Black Theology and Hermeneutical Methodology

Cone's exegetical suspicion is made manifest in his hermeneutical point of departure, "debunking" white supremacist notions that slavery and Christianity are consistent. Black Theology's answer to the question of hermeneutics can be stated briefly: *The hermeneutical principle for an exegesis of the Scriptures is the revelation of God in Christ as the liberator of the oppressed from social oppression and to political struggle, wherein the poor recognize that their fight against poverty and injustice is not only consistent with the gospel but is the gospel of Jesus Christ.*[42]

Cone's exegetical suspicion also lead him to see in the hermeneutical methodology of white supremacy a treatment of salvation that either divorced it from sociopolitical liberation or made it a secondary concern. Cone, however, moves quickly to dispel the notion of the legitimacy of the biblical hermeneutics of white supremacists by asserting that "any starting point that ignores God in Christ as the Liberator of the oppressed or that makes salvation as liberation secondary is *ipso facto* invalid and thus heretical."[43] Thus, for Cone, the validity of any starting point for a proper hermeneutical methodology lies in its departure from the biblical witness that God reveals Godself in a condition of oppression as a liberator of oppressed peoples. According to Cone:

> The test of the validity of this starting point, although dialectically related to black cultural experience, is not found in the particularity of the oppressed culture alone. It is found in the One who freely granted us freedom when we were doomed to slavery. In God's revelation in Scripture we come to the

[41] Taken from ibid., 61.

[42] James H. Cone, *God of the Oppressed* (San Francisco: Harper & Row, 1975) 81–2.

[43] Ibid., 82.

recognition that the divine liberation of the oppressed is not determined by our perceptions but by the God of the Exodus, the prophets, and Jesus Christ who calls the oppressed into a liberated existence. Divine revelation alone is the test of the validity of this starting point.[44]

Therefore, for Cone, the biblical emphasis on God's revelation as the sociopolitical liberation of the oppressed informs contemporary theology in the following ways. (1) There can be no Christian theology that is not social and political. If theology is to speak about the God of Jesus who reveals Godself in the struggle of the oppressed for freedom, then theology must also become political, speaking for the God of the poor and the oppressed. (2) The biblical emphasis on God's continuing act of liberation in the present and future means that theology cannot merely repeat what the Bible says or what is found in a particular theological tradition. Theology must be prophetic, recognizing the relativity of human speech, but also that God can use human speech at a particular time for the proclamation of God's Word to the suffering poor. (3) Theology cannot ignore the tradition. While the tradition is not the gospel, it is the bearer of an interpretation of the gospel at a particular point in time. By studying the tradition, we not only gain insight into a particular past time but also into our own time as the past and present meet dialectically. For only through this dialectical encounter with the tradition are we given the freedom to move beyond it. (4) Theology is always a word about the liberation of the oppressed and the humiliated. It is a word of judgment for the oppressors and the rulers. Whenever theologians fail to make this point unmistakably clear, they are not doing Christian theology but the theology of the Antichrist.[45]

Indeed, for Cone, white theology has been the Antichrist insofar as its theological presuppositions have emerged out of white culture rather than biblical revelation. The latter speaks to the poor and downtrodden in a situation of oppression, according to Cone, letting them know that their struggle for liberation is the essence of divine activity while the former conceives of biblical history as condoning slavery and seeks to justify black enslavement by treating it as a continuation of that history.

Herein, for Cone, lies the ideological nature of white theology. Its inability to transcend its culture, a culture of human enslavement and not of human freedom, puts it in direct opposition to the God of the Exodus, the prophets, and Jesus Christ. Since white theology has not transcended the axiological perspective of white culture, we must conclude that white theology is an ideological distortion of the gospel of Jesus.[46]

---

[44] Ibid.
[45] See ibid., 82–3.
[46] Ibid., 96–7.

In Cone's judgment, reinterpreting theology out of its ideological trappings requires that we raise the methodological question, "What is Christ's relation to human culture?" Given, for Cone, that the response to this question is always contextual, he lifts up America and God's relation to black and white cultures as an example.

> God's relation to black and white cultures in America is not identical. When it is considered, on the one hand, that George Washington, Thomas Jefferson, and Richard Nixon are representatives of the white way of life, and on the other hand, that the biblical God is the God whose will is disclosed in the liberation of slaves, then the divine relationship to white culture is obvious. The biblical God stands in opposition to the culture of slave masters, who idolatrously usurp the power to define humanity on the assumption of white superiority.[47]

Thus, Cone sees white theology as idolatrous insofar as it seeks to do theology on the basis of white supremacy rather than human equality, and in so doing contradicts the biblical witness. This is why Cone deems it a theological necessity to destroy the relationship between white culture and theological reflection.

> This is due, not so much to the bad intentions of particular white theologians as it is to the social context in which their thinking occurs. Indeed, because the values of white culture are antithetical to biblical revelation it is impossible to be white (culturally speaking) and also think biblically.[48]

To think biblically, according to Cone, is to think liberation, and to think liberation is to transcend the ideological nuances of white culture. Therefore, for Cone,

> Biblical thinking is *liberated* thought, i.e., thinking that is not entrapped by social categories of the dominant culture. If white theologians are to understand this thought process, they must undergo a conversion wherein they are given, by the Holy Spirit, a new way of thinking and acting in the world, defined and limited by God's will to liberate the oppressed. To think biblically is to think in the light of the liberating interest of the oppressed. Any other starting point is a contradiction of the social a priori of the Scripture.[49]

This means that any relevant hermeneutical methodology, in Cone's judgment, must depart from the social condition of humanity in general and the oppressed in particular. Biblical revelation, for Cone, is inextricably bound with God's speaking into a particular historical condition of oppression with the intention of eradicating that oppression. This is why Cone has little patience with the criticism that Black Theology is nothing more than a psy-

---

[47] Ibid., 96.
[48] Ibid., 97.
[49] Ibid.

chological need of black people in an existential reality of acute suffering. Rather, for Cone, the identification of liberation with God's revelation is the central theme of the Bible and is therefore not derived from human needs. Christian theology does not move from human needs to God, but from God's revelation to our needs.[50]

This view of God, for Cone, emerges out of the biblical portrayal of God as a liberator of oppressed people in both the Exodus and the Incarnation. More importantly, according to Cone, by God making Godself known in the Bible as a liberator, one cannot speak meaningfully about God without speaking of the liberation of all oppressed people as the essence of divine activity. Cone constructs two hermeneutical principles in speaking of Black Theology and the Christian understanding of God: (1) The Christian understanding of God arises from the biblical view of revelation, a revelation of God that takes place in the liberation of oppressed Israel and is completed in God's becoming man in Jesus Christ. This means that whatever is said about the nature of God and God's being-in-the-world must be based on the biblical account of God's revelatory activity. (2) The doctrine of God in Black Theology must be the God who is participating in the liberation of the oppressed of the land. This hermeneutical principle arises out of the first. Because God has made Godself known in the history of oppressed Israel and decisively in the Oppressed One, who is Jesus Christ, it is impossible to say anything about God without seeing God as being involved in the contemporary liberation of all oppressed people. The God of Black Theology is the God of and for the oppressed of the land who makes Godself known through their liberation. Any other view is a denial of the biblical revelation.[51]

While Cone concedes that there are themes other than liberation in the Bible, he also argues that liberation from sociopolitical oppression is the central theme of Scripture. Therefore, it should be the point of departure of any relevant hermeneutical methodology.

Black Theology, Hermeneutical Methodology, and the Old Testament

Regarding the Old Testament, the Exodus narrative serves as the cornerstone of Cone's hermeneutical methodology. It affirms, for Cone, the biblical view of salvation as one of liberation from sociopolitical oppression, thus striking at the very heart of white distortions of the gospel.

> It seems clear to me that whatever else we may say about Scripture, it is first and foremost a story of Israelite people who believed that Yahweh was involved in their history. In the Old Testament, the story begins with the first

[50] Ibid., 99.

[51] James H. Cone, *A Black Theology of Liberation* (New York: Lippincott, 1970) 116.

Exodus of Hebrew slaves from Egypt and continues through the second Exodus from Babylon and the rebuilding of the Temple. To be sure, there are many ways to look at this story, but the import of the biblical message is clear on this point: God's salvation is revealed in the liberation of slaves from socio-political bondage.[52]

Therefore, the task of theology, according to Cone, is to interpret the meaning of human existence in a particular historical context, identifying the struggle of the oppressed for liberation with God's own struggle as revealed in the Bible in general and the Exodus narrative in particular. God's promise to take up the cause of the oppressed assures the oppressed of liberation, a promise God makes not only to Israel but to all oppressed peoples.

> I have heard the groaning of the people of Israel whom the Egyptians hold in bondage and I have remembered my covenant. Say therefore to the people of Israel, "I am the Lord, and I will bring you out from under the burdens of the Egyptians, and I will deliver you from their bondage, and I will redeem you with an outstretched arm and with great acts of judgment, and I will take you for my people, and I will be your God" (Exod 6:5-7a).[53]

Cone moves quickly to point out that the identification of the oppressed's struggle with God's struggle does not represent oppressed strivings for inner contentment. Rather, the identification is derived from the concrete historical struggle of both Israelite and black communities. It is only in this context, for Cone, that the validity of the faith of both communities can be understood.

> Whatever may be said about the biblical faith and black faith derived from Scripture, neither was based on a feeling of inwardness separated from historical experiences. Both Israel and later the black community took history seriously and continued to test the validity of their faith in the context of historical struggle. Indeed, the faith of Israel and of black people was an historical faith, that is, a trust in the faithfulness and loyalty of God in the midst of historical troubles.[54]

Thus, in Cone's view, the origin of faith for both communities is not to be found in their subjective consciousness, but in the revelatory movement of God in the midst of their historical struggles.

This is why, for Cone, there is no freedom that is not realized in history. He sees history as the arena in which dialectically oppression and liberation meet. It is the medium wherein biblical revelation transforms social existence by affirming that human enslavement is antithetical to God's will and further affirming the struggle of the oppressed to free themselves.

[52] James H. Cone, *Speaking the Truth* (Grand Rapids, Mich.: Eerdmans, 1986) 5.
[53] Cone, *God of the Oppressed,* 99.
[54] Ibid., 100.

There is no freedom without transformation, i.e., without the struggle for liberation in this world. There is no freedom without the commitment of a revolutionary praxis against injustice, slavery and oppression. Freedom then is not merely a thought in my head; it is the socio-historical movement of a people from oppression to liberation—Israelites from Egypt, Black people from American slavery. It is the mind and body in motion, responding to the passion and the rhythm of divine revelation, and affirming that no chain shall hold my humanity down.[55]

For Cone, then, human salvation is revealed in the Old Testament as being a historical phenomenon that is inextricably linked with God's righteousness in delivering the oppressed from political bondage. The liberation event was realized in the Israelite exodus from Egypt and is the basis upon which black people assert that God will do the same for them. Thus, for both communities, YHWH is seen as the Savior because "the Lord saved [her] that day from the hand of the Egyptians; and Israel saw the Egyptians dead upon the seashore" (Exod 14:30).[56] This is why the Israelites sang:

> I will sing to the Lord, for [the Lord] has risen up in triumph;
> the house and this rider [the Lord] has hurled into the sea.
> The Lord is my refuge and my defense,
> [the Lord] has shown [the Lord's self] my deliverer (Exod 15:1-2).[57]

The Israelites understood that the revelation of God is one of liberation of oppressed people from sociopolitical bondage and that this activity is synonymous with human salvation.

Black Theology, Hermeneutical Methodology, and the New Testament

For Cone, Scripture as the story of sociopolitical liberation also applies to the New Testament. The story of historical salvation is continued in the New Testament with the difference being that it moves from the particular in the Old Testament to the universal in the New Testament. Indeed, Christians affirm that the New Testament is the witness to the fulfillment of God's drama of salvation begun with Israel's liberation from Egypt.[58] As the basis for his assertion Cone cites the Matthean account of Jesus' proclamation that he did not come to abolish the Law and the prophets but to complete it. Further, Cone argues that the New Testament writers saw the God of Jesus as the God of Abraham, Isaac, and Jacob, and that through the Incarnation

---

[55] James H. Cone, "Freedom, History and Hope," *The Journal of the Interdenominational Theological Center* 1 (Fall 1973) 60.

[56] Ibid.

[57] Ibid. For a more elaborate treatment of Cone's hermeneutical methodology, particularly the prophetic books, see *God of the Oppressed*, 68ff.

[58] Cone, *God of the Oppressed*, 72.

God reveals Godself in the man Jesus as an impoverished Jew. In so doing, God continually identifies with the oppressed and against oppressors. The Christ-event, for Cone, however, is more. On the one hand, Jesus is the continuation of the Law and the prophets; on the other, he is the inauguration of a completely new age, and his words and deeds are signs of its imminent coming.[59]

Like pro-slavery ideologues, Cone sees the New Testament as a continuation of the Old Testament. Unlike pro-slavery advocates, the meaning of the New Testament, in Cone's view, lies in its taking the theme of liberation to universal dimensions. The meaning of Jesus is found in God's will to make liberation not simply the property of one people but of all humankind.[60] Hence, for Cone, Jesus did not see himself as a prophet, warning of the advent of the coming age, but as the One who brings that age into being: "through [Jesus'] words and deeds, he became the *inaugurator* of the Kingdom, which is bound up with his person as disclosed in his identification with the poor."[61] Cone cites Jesus' proclamation following his baptism (Mark 1:11; Matt 3:17; Luke 3:22) as the basis for his contention that Jesus understood himself to be the inaugurator of the kingdom.

Cone then connects the passages above with Psalm 2:7 and Isaiah 42:1 in establishing Jesus' awareness of his role of kingship in the context of servanthood: "You are my son, I become your father" (Ps 2:7); "Here is my servant, whom I uphold, my chosen one in whom I delight, I have bestowed my spirit upon him, and he will make justice shine on the nations" (Isa 42:1).[62] Cone then explains the implications of these passages for the oppressed:

> Psalm 2:7, a coronation hymn, emphasizes [Jesus'] role as King, who is God's representative to bring justice to the nations. Isaiah 42:1 refers to the Servant of Yahweh, who brings justice by his own suffering. Jesus' synthesis of these two themes produced a new messianic image. Servanthood provides the context for exercising kingship or lordship. The King is a Servant who suffers on behalf of the people. He takes their pain and affliction upon himself, thereby redeeming them from oppression and for freedom. Here, then we have the key to Jesus' understanding of his mission: Lordship and Servanthood together, that is, the establishment of justice through suffering.[63]

Therefore, for Cone, the primary point of these narratives is not Jesus' rejection of a revolutionary messiahship (pro-slavery advocates), but *"Jesus' rejection of any role that would separate him from the poor."*[64]

[59] Ibid.
[60] Cone, *Speaking the Truth*, 5.
[61] Cone, *God of the Oppressed*, 74.
[62] Both passages taken from ibid.
[63] Ibid., 74–5.
[64] Ibid.

The theme of God's liberation for the poor reaches its pinnacle in the ministry of Jesus in his proclamation of Isaiah 61:1-2 in the Nazareth synagogue:

> The spirit of the Lord is upon me because he has anointed me,
> he has sent me to announce good news to the poor,
> to proclaim release for prisoners, and recovery of sight for the blind;
> to let the broken victims go free,
> to proclaim the year of the Lord's favour.[65]

Jesus then connects this passage to his own ministry, according to Cone, by commenting, "Today in your very hearing, this text has come true."

Therefore, for Cone, "[Jesus] is God [Godself] coming into the very depths of human existence for the sole purpose of striking off the chains of slavery, thereby freeing [humanity] from ungodly principalities and powers that hinder [their] relationship[s] with God."[66] This is why Cone sees the freeing of humans from all earthly mediums of enslavement and the inauguration of the kingdom as one and the same event. Indeed, the message of the kingdom strikes at the very center of humanity's desire to define their own existences in the light of their own interests at the price of their fellow humans' enslavement.[67] According to Cone, the kingdom is the advent of a new age—an age of liberation wherein God acts in history on behalf of the oppressed for its salvation. For Cone, this means that the message of the kingdom is not a complex phenomenon to be deciphered only by the erudite. Rather, the kingdom is a manifestation of God's disdain for the institutionalization of ideologies as a means of furthering the interests of oppressors. The kingdom, for Cone,

> is a message about the ghetto and all other injustices done in the name of democracy and religion to further the social, political and economic interests of the oppressor. In Christ, God enters human affairs and takes sides with the oppressed. Their suffering becomes [God's]; their despair, divine despair. Through Christ, the poor [human] is offered freedom now to rebel against that which makes him [or her] other than human.[68]

By seeing the intimate connection between the advent of the kingdom and the exposing of religio-political ideologies, Cone is able to connect the kingdom to the black experience in America and Black Power in particular, in other words, the ability of blacks to struggle for liberation by whatever means the black community deems necessary. In Cone's view, the kingdom

---

[65] Taken from ibid. See also Luke 4:18-19.

[66] James H. Cone, *Black Theology and Black Power*, Twentieth Anniversary Edition (San Francisco: Harper & Row, 1989) 35.

[67] Ibid., 35–6.

[68] Ibid., 36.

makes the struggle of the oppressed God's own. Because Black Power is the medium through which black people in America affirm their humanity, being what God intended, then the will of God and the purpose of Black Power are synonymous. Cone likens this to what Jurgen Moltmann refers to as the "political hermeneutics of the gospel." According to Moltmann:

> One cannot grasp freedom in faith without hearing simultaneously the categorical imperative: One must serve through bodily, social and political obedience the liberation of the suffering creation out of real affliction. . . . Consequently, the missionary proclamation of the cross of the Resurrected One is not an opium of the people which intoxicates and incapacitates, but the ferment of new freedom. It leads to the awaking of that revolt which, in the "power of resurrection" . . . follows the categorical imperative to overthrow all conditions in which [humanity] is a being who labors and is heavily laden.[69]

This establishes, for Cone, that the gospel is not an opiate, but frees those who are victims of sociopolitical oppression to struggle for freedom recognizing that one is not human until one is free. More importantly, according to Cone, "If the gospel of Christ, as Moltmann suggests, frees a [human] to be for those who labor and are heavily laden, the humiliated and abused, then it would seem that for twentieth century America the message of Black Power is the message of Christ himself."[70]

Conclusion

We began the chapter by examining the hermeneutical methodology of white supremacy. We saw that it principally sought to establish that God ordained slavery, and that it is part of the natural order of human relationships. It also sought to use the Hamitic hypothesis to justify human enslavement and argue for its eternal nature. Further, the hermeneutical methodology of white supremacy saw the etymological derivation of the name Ham (meaning black or burnt) as the basis for its contention that God intended for blacks to be slaves and whites to be their masters. It saw Jesus' and Paul's omissions of institutional slavery as sinful as implicit approval of slavery. Finally, the hermeneutical methodology of white supremacy conceived of salvation only in ethereal terms and not in sociopolitical terms.

We then examined the hermeneutical methodology of Black Theology. We illuminated its exegetical suspicion, showing that the biblical witness conceives of salvation in sociopolitical terms. We analyzed Black Theology's treatment of the Exodus narrative in the Old Testament and Jesus' proclamation of his ministry in the Nazareth synagogue in the New Testament, es-

---

[69] Quoted in ibid., 37. Taken from Moltmann, "Toward a Political Hermeneutics of the Gospel," *Union Seminary Quarterly Review* 23:4 (Summer 1968) 313–4.

[70] Ibid.

tablishing that God does not condone slavery but that God's revelation in Jesus Christ is one of human freedom. Finally, we showed that Black Theology establishes an inextricable link between the advent of the kingdom and the exposing of religio-political ideologies by connecting the kingdom to the Black Power movement and the strivings of blacks to expose the hermeneutical methodology of white supremacy as antithetical to God's will, freeing blacks to struggle for their liberation by whatever means they deem appropriate. Because Cone uses his exegetical suspicion in recognizing that "the prevailing view of scripture does not take important pieces of data into account," that the hermeneutical methodology of white supremacy represents an ideological distortion of the Bible, and that a new hermeneutical methodology rooted in sociopolitical liberation needed to be constructed to effectively destroy the credibility of white supremacist hermeneutical claims, he passes the third stage of Segundo's hermeneutic circle.

CHAPTER 4

A New Hermeneutic

The fourth stage of the hermeneutic circle is our new hermeneutic, "our new way of interpreting the fountainhead of our faith (i.e., Scripture) with the new elements at our disposal."[1] For Black Theology, that new hermeneutic is: "blackness is at once the symbol of oppression and of the certainty of liberation."[2] It is the theological assertion that God's revelation in "moments of oppression" as a liberator means that, in contemporary America, God identifies with oppressed blacks and participates in their struggle for liberation. And because God both identifies with black oppression and participates in black liberation, the attainment of liberation is assured. This is the meaning of blackness as a symbolic form of both oppression and liberation at the same time. It represents the primary presupposition of Black Theology and the basis upon which Cone treats the doctrines of the faith. Cone rests the authority of this approach on the common experience of black oppression and strivings for liberation in America. Thus, for Cone, the validity of any doctrinal treatment lies in its ability to enhance the liberation struggle of black people, that is, to reveal the essence of blackness as expressed in Black Power. This is why, according to Cone:

> If the doctrine is compatible with or enhances the drive for black freedom, then it is the gospel of Jesus Christ. If the doctrine is against or indifferent to the essence of blackness as expressed in Black Power, then it is the work of the Antichrist. It is as simple as that.[3]

Therefore, in Cone's view, any relevant systematic theology must interpret doctrines such that it equates the gospel with the freedom of black people.

> Black Theology is not prepared to discuss the doctrine of God, [Humanity], Christ, Church, Holy Spirit—the whole spectrum of Christian theology—

[1] Juan Luis Segundo, *The Liberation of Theology,* trans. John Drury (Maryknoll, N.Y.: Orbis Books, 1976) 9.

[2] James H. Cone, *A Black Theology of Liberation,* Twentieth Anniversary Edition (Maryknoll, N.Y.: Orbis Books, 1990) 182–3.

[3] James H. Cone, *Black Theology and Black Power,* Twentieth Anniversary Edition (San Francisco: Harper & Row, 1989) 121.

without making each doctrine an analysis of the emancipation of black people. It believes that, in this time, moment and situation, all Christian doctrines must be interpreted in such a manner that they unreservedly say something to black people who are living under unbearable oppression.[4]

Put more simply, this means that Black Theology stands in opposition to any doctrinal treatment that does not take into account the black demand for freedom now.

The next task is to examine this new hermeneutic in Cone's theology by looking at the doctrines of God, humanity, Christ, eschatology, and revolution and violence.

God

For Cone, "The point of departure of Black Theology is the biblical God as [God] is related to the black liberation struggle. It asks, 'How do we dare speak of God in a suffering world, a world in which blacks are humiliated because they are black?'"[5] Cone sees this starting point as inextricably bound with his view of the God-language of white religion. He sees it as an instrument of black enslavement by justifying slavery theologically and inducing in black people an anti-revolutionary spirit. This is why, in Cone's judgment, the God of white religion is an idol insofar as it stands in opposition to the nature of the God of the Bible, that is, as a liberator. Therefore, the destruction of the white God is an inescapable task in Black Theology and the realization of black liberation.

> That the God-language of white religion has been used to create a docile spirit among black people while whites aggressively attacked them is beyond question. But that does not mean that we cannot kill the white God, so that the God of black people can make [God's] presence known in the black-white encounter. The white God is an idol, created by racist bastards, and we black people must perform the iconoclastic task of smashing false images.[6]

According to Cone, this is made possible by God's revelation. God reveals to oppressed peoples not only who God is, but that the oppressed must destroy those instruments in society that deny them their freedom. For oppressed black people in America, that instrument is whiteness. Put another way, "Through Christ, black people have come to know not only who he is but also who they are, and what they must do about that which would make them nothings."[7] This is why, for Cone, speaking of God in a suffering world in which blacks are oppressed because they are black

---

[4] Ibid.
[5] Cone, *A Black Theology of Liberation*, 115.
[6] Ibid., 114.
[7] Cone, *Black Theology and Black Power*, 120–1.

occupies the central place in our theological perspective, [and] forces us to say nothing about God that does not participate in the emancipation of black people. God-talk is not Christian talk unless it is *directly* related to the liberation of the oppressed. Any other talk is at best an intellectual hobby, and at worst blasphemy.[8]

Therefore, any relevant treatment of God must, according to Cone, depart from the God of the Bible and not the God of white culture. Cone sees the former as departing from the liberation of oppressed peoples wherein the latter departs from the appropriateness of black enslavement by whites.

In so doing, Cone recognizes the ideological nature of white religion by conceiving of God as a God of all peoples who approves of the existing situation and is therefore not interested in sociopolitical liberation. It represents, for Cone, an "ideological ruse" for perpetuating the interests of white culture making white assertions about God the work of the Antichrist.

> When George Washington, Thomas Jefferson, Lyndon Johnson, Richard Nixon and other "great" Americans can invoke the name of God at the same time they are defining the society for white people only, Black Theology knows that it cannot approach the God-question too casually. It must ask, "How can we speak of God without being associated with the oppressed of the land."[9]

Cone responds by conceiving of blackness as God's intention for humanity which means in ideological terms the destruction of whiteness. The goal of Black Theology is the destruction of everything white so that black people can be liberated from alien gods.[10] Thus, by recognizing the destruction of whiteness as a necessary precondition for black liberation, Black Theology is said to be in a process of deideologization.

Further, Cone is also aware of the ideological nature of white religion in its conception of God as colorblind in a society where black people suffer because they are black.

> There is no place in Black Theology for a colorless God in a society when people suffer precisely because of their color. The black theologian must reject any conception of God which stifles black self-determination by picturing God as a God of all peoples. Either God is identified with the oppressed to the point that their experience becomes [God's] or [God] is a God of racism.[11]

However, for Cone, because God has made the goal of black people God's own (liberation from white oppression), Black Theology believes that it is

[8] Cone, *A Black Theology of Liberation*, 115.
[9] Ibid., 109.
[10] Ibid., 118.
[11] Ibid., 120–1.

not only appropriate but necessary to begin the doctrine of God with an insistence on God's blackness.[12]

Cone further disassociates Black Theology from white culture by identifying God's selection of Israel as God's chosen people. By electing Israelite slaves as God's people and by becoming the Oppressed One in Jesus Christ, God discloses to humanity that God is known where humans experience humiliation and suffering.[13] More importantly, it means that "[God's] election of Israel and incarnation in Christ reveal that the *liberation* of the oppressed is a part of the innermost nature of God [Godself]. This means that liberation is not an afterthought but the essence of divine activity."[14] This is significant, for Cone, in that it biblically establishes God's identification with and participation in the liberation struggle of oppressed peoples.

White theologians, according to Cone, have historically treated the concept of liberation by either insisting on the dangers involved in talking about color or that liberation is God's nature but that it applies to Scripture and not the contemporary situation.

> To be sure, they would *probably* concede that the concept of liberation is essential to the biblical view of God. But it is still impossible for them to translate the biblical emphasis on liberation to the black-white struggle today. Invariably, they quibble on this issue, moving from side to side, always pointing out the dangers of extremism on both sides. They really cannot make a decision, because it has been made already for them. The way in which scholars would analyze God and black people was decided when black slaves were brought to this land, while [churchgoers] sang "Jesus, Lover of My Soul."[15]

In fact, Cone sees a direct correlation between white theologians today and those during slavery. Both, for Cone, speak of black freedom in spiritual but not material terms. Although contemporary white theologians, according to Cone, have a more erudite way of speaking of God's concern for all humanity, including blacks, "they go on to talk about God and secularization or some other white problem unrelated to [the] emancipation of black people. This style is a contemporary white way of saying that, 'Christianity . . . does not make the least alteration in civil property.'"[16] Therefore, for Cone, the destruction of the white God and the exaltation of the black God require that all of humanity, including whites, take the side of the oppressed and participate with them in the process of liberation. It means that *"we must become black with God!"*[17]

[12] Ibid., 121.
[13] Ibid.
[14] Ibid.
[15] Ibid., 123.
[16] Ibid.
[17] Ibid., 124.

Naturally this begs the question, "How can white people become black?" Cone distinguishes between a physiological blackness and an ontological blackness. The former refers to black people in America who have been the victims of white racist hegemony. And because of this, Black Theology sees them as the sole source of revelation in the world. In so being, Christian theology, for Cone, cannot speak of God without departing from the black experience in America. The latter is an ontological symbol for all people who participate in the liberation of humanity from oppression. Thus, physiological blackness represents the particular dimension of Black Theology while ontological blackness represents its universal dimension.

Therefore, in Cone's judgment, blackness is not just the race of a particular group of people, but an ontological way of being in the world—a way of being in the world that is indispensable in bringing about human salvation. Thus, becoming black, for Cone, is a gift from God and not humanity.

> The question "How can white people become black?" is analogous to the Philippian jailer's question to Paul and Silas, "What must I do to be saved?" The implication is that if we work hard enough at it, we can reach the goal. But the misunderstanding here is the failure to see that blackness or salvation (the two are synonymous) is the work of God and not [humanity]. It is not something we accomplish; it is a gift.[18]

Further, for Cone, this gift makes humans completely new creatures in Christ, producing in them a disdain for sociopolitical oppression and efforts to justify it and a profound desire to participate with the oppressed in the liberation struggle. Therefore, the recognition of religio-political ideologies and the yearning to destroy their influence for the sake of human freedom are synonymous with the will of God. For Cone, this gift of God to humans represents the true meaning of God as Wholly Other. God comes to us in God's blackness, which is wholly unlike whiteness, and to receive God's revelation is to become black with God by joining God's work of liberation.[19] This is what the Christian view of God means for Black Theology.

What does the blackness of God mean for those who are the recipients of God's liberating activity? It is to an examination of Black Theology's treatment of humanity that we now turn.

Humanity

Cone's treatment of humanity departs from the existential reality of concrete human oppression. To speak of humanity, for Cone, is to speak of one's "being-in-the-world-of-human-oppression." It is in this context, Cone contends, that God reveals Godself as a transcendent God who enters into

---

[18] Ibid., 124–5.
[19] Ibid., 125.

human history, transforming human oppression into divine liberation. Thus, Cone recognizes that while theology departs from God, one can speak of God only as God is related to the transformation of human relationships.

> We know who God is not because we can move beyond our finiteness but because the transcendent God has become immanent in our history, transforming human events into divine events of liberation. It is the divine involvement in historical events of liberation that makes theology God-centered; but because God participates in [humanity's] historical liberation, we can only speak of God as [God] is related to [humanity]. In this sense, theology is anthropology.[20]

This means, for Cone, that eternity breaks into time for the purpose of usurping human oppression with divine liberation.

The oppressed are the sole source of revelation, according to Cone, insofar as they have been the bearers of white injustice enabling them, by virtue of that injustice, to experience the liberating power of God. For Cone, "only the oppressed know what [humanity] is because they have encountered both the depravity of human behavior from the oppressors and also the healing powers as revealed in the Oppressed One."[21] Further, Cone asserts that this liberating power of God infuses in the oppressed a spirit of liberation and informs them that its struggle for liberation is the ultimate expression of human freedom. This is why Cone sees only the oppressed as being truly free.

The concreteness of human existence, for Cone, reveals to humanity that sociopolitical oppression is a denial of human freedom and that, in such a context, true humanity is measured by one's identification with the victims of that oppression. Being human is the same as being against evil by joining sides with those who are victims of evil.[22] "Quite literally, it means becoming oppressed with the oppressed, making their cause our cause by involving ourselves in the liberation struggle. *No [human] is free until all [humans] are free.*"[23]

For the oppressed in particular, Cone argues that its oppressive context compels them to construct a value system opposite that of an oppressive society. Therefore, for Cone, the meaning of freedom for the oppressed is clear: "They are forced by the very nature of their condition to interpret their existence in the world contrary to the value-structures of the oppressor's society. For the oppressed, to be is to be in revolt against the forces that impede the creation of the new [human]."[24] In light of this, Cone sees

---

[20] Ibid., 151.
[21] Ibid., 159.
[22] Ibid., 160.
[23] Ibid.
[24] Ibid., 162.

human freedom not as an abstract question unrelated to concrete human suffering, but as a confrontation by the oppressed against the oppressors with the former demanding that the latter see them as an "I" rather than a "Thou." To be free, contends Cone, is for the oppressed to demand that the society see them as free human beings and not to conform to societal depictions of their humanity.

To be sure, Cone understands that human suffering is inevitable in the liberation process. He understands that in the aftermath of such a confrontation, oppressors will invariably use their control of the dispensation of sociopolitical power to destroy the credibility of the oppressed's struggle, particularly its leaders.

> The intention is to demonstrate the perversity of the rebel's involvement by picturing him [or her] as the destroyer of the "good." At no time is the rebel given the opportunity to define his [or her] way of looking at the world, because the mass media belongs to the oppressors who will not permit the seditious presence to extend itself.[25]

If the oppressed persist in confronting the source of its injustice, for Cone, oppressors will use their power to deprive the oppressed of the exigencies of life. More particularly, asserts Cone, if oppressors are unable to convince the oppressed of the legitimacy of the existing situation theoretically, they will impose the situation on the oppressed through economic reprisal and/or social ostracism.

> When the rulers first perceive that one is a menace to the society, their initial response is to try to silence the undesirable by cutting off the sources of physical existence and social involvement. This is to remind the rebel who's boss. The oppressors hope that by making it difficult to live, the rebel will come around to seeing the world the way rulers view it.[26]

This is why Cone describes the black experience in America as an absurd one. Absurd because of the pain associated with being black in white America and facing the prospects of economic reprisal or physical death in the attempt to transform it.

> Growing up in America is an absurd experience for black people. At first, one does not know what is going on. He [or she] cannot figure out what he [or she] has done to merit the treatment accorded him [or her]. But then he [or she] realizes that white brutality is not related to his [or her] particular actions. It is white society's way of telling the black man [or woman] that he [or she] is not a person. Now he [or she] must make a decision: either accept his [or her] place or resolve to call down upon himself [or herself] the nothingness of white existence by revolting against the world as it is.[27]

[25] Ibid., 176–7.
[26] Ibid., 176.
[27] Ibid., 178.

The decision to do the latter (revolting against the world as it is) is the meaning of an eschatological decision for black liberation (Chapter 1).

Cone sees a correlation between human suffering and the biblical witness. God's selection of Israel, according to Cone, means that God has not only called them to share in liberation but also to the "terrible responsibility" of fighting against everything that is against that liberation. Therefore, Cone sees the unfolding of the history of Israel as the movement of God's liberating activity in the world.

The same holds true, for Cone, in regard to the life of Jesus. He chose an existence of suffering and persecution for the freedom of humanity. Thus, Cone maintains that one cannot reasonably assert that one is a follower of Jesus and condone the enslavement of human beings. Further evidence of Jesus' identification with the oppressed, according to Cone, is his specification of the kingdom being only for the poor insofar as they represent the meaning of oppression and the certainty of liberation.

> The very character of human existence as defined in his life is enough to show that we cannot be for Jesus and for societal humiliation of human beings. To be for him means being for the oppressed as expressed in their self-determination. Jesus himself expresses this by limiting the Kingdom to the poor because they represent the meaning of oppression and the certainty of liberation.[28]

In regard to the black-white encounter in America, freedom, in Cone's judgment, is the affirmation of blackness in a society founded on whiteness. It means identifying with blacks in their fight against whiteness, that is, human enslavement. It is to live one's life seeking to transcend the limitations imposed by white society.

> To be free is to be black, that is, identified with the victims of humiliation in human society and a participant in the liberation of [humanity]. The free man [or woman] in America is the man [or woman] who does not tolerate whiteness but fights against it knowing that it is the source of human misery. The free man [or woman] is the black man [or woman] living in an alien world but refusing to behave according to its expectations.[29]

Therefore, for Cone, to be free in America is to accept blackness as the only way of existing in the world.

Cone also conceives of the human as a fallen creature. He sees the biblical narrative of the Fall as Israel's view of universal sin and is therefore comprehensible only to them. Thus, Cone contends that universal sin is defined by each community and is largely determined by the sources that that community deems to be indispensable in theological reflection. Therefore, in

---

[28] Ibid., 181–2.
[29] Ibid., 183.

Cone's judgment, Israel is in a state of fallenness not because of Adam and Eve per se, but because she did not define her existence according to divine liberation. Sin then is the failure of Israel to recognize the liberating work of God.[30] It is to deny the liberating work of God and to define one's existence according to societal standards. It is to pursue a meaningful existence within the limitations of an oppressive society.

> Sin then is a condition of human existence in which [humanity] denies the essence of God's liberating activity as revealed in Jesus Christ. It is a way of life in which [humanity] ceases to be [humanity] and makes choices according to his [or her] private interests, identifying the ultimate with an alien power. It is accepting slavery as a condition of human existence by denying the freedom which is grounded in God's activity. Sin is an alienation from the source of humanity in the world, resulting in human oppression and misery.[31]

When applied to contemporary America, Black Theology believes that a universal treatment of sin that is meaningful to both black and white people is not possible. For Cone, sin is meaningful only to an oppressed community in its struggle for liberation, in other words, it is perceived "only in the moment of oppression and liberation." This means, for Cone, that

> black people, like Israel of old, know what sin is because they have experienced the source of their being and are now able to analyze their own existence in relation to the world at large. They know what nonbeing (sin) is because they have experienced being (Black Power). We are now in a position to say what the world ought to be in relation to what it is.[32]

Therefore, according to Cone, since sin is perceived only in "the moment of oppression and liberation," it is inextricably bound with revelation insofar as it occurs only in "moments of oppression." Since sin is inseparable from revelation and since revelation is an event that takes place in the moment of liberation from oppression, there can be no knowledge of the sinful condition except in the movement of an oppressed community claiming its freedom.[33] Further, Cone asserts that just as the oppressed are the only real source of revelation, only the oppressed know what sin is "because they are both the victims of evil and the recipients of God's liberating activity." They are both "the symbol of oppression and of the certainty of liberation."

Finally, for Cone, sin for white people is the creation of a culture that is fundamentally racist. It is condoning the enslavement of blacks and the extermination of Indians. In a word, sin is whiteness—white people's desire to be God in human relations.[34]

[30] Ibid., 198.
[31] Ibid., 190.
[32] Ibid., 190–1.
[33] Ibid., 191.
[34] Ibid., 193.

Sin for black people is their desire to be white and not black. It is to lose one's black identity in a world permeated with whiteness. Most importantly, it is accepting white definitions of black humanity.

> Sin for black people is the loss of identity. It is saying Yes to the white absurd-ity—accepting the world as it is by letting white people define black exist-ence. To be in sin is to be contented with white solutions for the "black problem" and not rebelling against every infringement of white being on black being.[35]

Our task now lies in an analysis of the christology of Black Theology, examining how it reconciles divine and human activity and its relevance to black liberation.

Jesus Christ

The point of departure for Cone's Christology is, "What does Christ mean for the oppressed blacks of the land?" The answer to this question, for Cone, lies in a dialectical relationship between biblical revelation and social context. In particular, Cone sees the authority of the Bible coupled with faith through divine grace as that which enables us in the twentieth century to appropriate biblical narratives concerning the historical struggle for free-dom in the first century for the purpose of transforming our reality.

> The authority of the Bible for Christology, therefore, does not lie in its ob-jective status as the literal Word of God. Rather, it is found in its power to point to the One whom the people have met in the historical struggle for freedom. Through the reading of Scripture, the people not only hear other stories about Jesus that enable them to move beyond the privateness of their own story; but through faith because of divine grace, they are taken from the present to the past and thrust back into their contemporary history with di-vine power to transform the sociopolitical context.[36]

This means, for Cone, that "through the experience of moving back and forth between the first and twentieth centuries, the Bible is transformed from just a report of what the disciples believed about Jesus to black people's personal story of God's will to liberate the oppressed in their con-temporary context."[37] Put another way, because Cone sees the Synoptic Gospels as revealing Jesus' life as a commitment to and identification with the poor and exploited and against those institutions that perpetuate human suffering, Jesus must also be identified with those who are the vic-tims of human suffering today. That people, for Cone, in contemporary

---

[35] Ibid., 196.

[36] James H. Cone, *God of the Oppressed* (San Francisco: Harper & Row, 1975) 112.

[37] Ibid., 112–3.

America is black people. Moreover, according to Cone, since Jesus identifies with the victims of societal injustice and since in the contemporary American context those victims are black, then the Jesus of the Bible is the Jesus of the black experience. For Cone, this is the meaning of the dialectical relationship between biblical revelation and social context.

> We must say unequivocally that who Jesus Christ is for black people today is found through an encounter with him in the social context of black existence. But as soon as that point is made, the other side of the paradox must be affirmed; otherwise the faith of the black experience is distorted. The Jesus of the black experience is the Jesus of Scripture. The dialectical relationship of the black experience and Scripture is the point of departure of Black Theology's Christology.[38]

Cone also sees this as the meaning of the black experience as the contemporary revelation of God (Chapter 1). If Jesus is revealed in the Bible as the One who came to set at liberty those who are oppressed, then in contemporary times where blacks are oppressed by whites, the revelation of God in Jesus can be found only in the black experience.

This dialectical relationship between biblical revelation and social context means that Black Theology places primary emphasis on Jesus' humanity. In this regard, Cone concurs with Pannenberg that christology must begin "from below" with the Jesus of history and not "from above" with the Divine Logos. Otherwise, for Cone, it allows for christological treatments divorced from concrete human suffering. This Cone sees as the fatal error of Docetism. By departing from Jesus' divinity rather than his humanity, Jesus' acts in history as a liberator were not seen as a legitimate medium for theological reflection. This point of departure played a primary role, according to Cone, in white theologians' and preachers' assertions that slavery and the gospel were consistent. Only by departing from Jesus' humanity in history, in Cone's view, are we able to establish that the Jesus of the Bible is the Jesus of the black experience, that is, to establish that Jesus is who he was.

> My assertion that "Jesus is who he was" affirms not only the importance of Scripture as the basis of Christology. It also stresses the biblical emphasis on Jesus' humanity in history as the starting point of christological analysis. For without the historical Jesus, theology is left with a docetic Christ who is said to be human but is actually nothing but an idea-principle in a theological system. We cannot have a human Christ unless we have a historical Christ, that is, unless we know his history. That is why the writers of the four Gospels tell the good news in the form of the story of Jesus' life. The events described are not intended as fiction but as God's way of changing the course of history in a human person.[39]

[38] Ibid., 113.
[39] Ibid., 118–9.

Focusing on the historical Jesus means that Black Theology recognizes history as the indispensable foundation of christology.[40]

Of equal significance, for Cone, was Jesus' Jewishness. While Cone recognizes the universal implications of the Christ-event, he also recognizes that God decided to reveal Godself to an oppressed Jewish people. According to Cone, this establishes not only God's identification with the oppressed but God's intention to make the oppressed's struggle God's own. In this regard, Cone contends that theologians cannot ignore the particularity of the incarnation. The particularity of Jesus' person as disclosed in his Jewishness is indispensable for christological analysis.[41] Thus, for Cone, Jesus' Jewishness was essential in effectuating God's will to liberate humanity in general and all oppressed peoples in particular. The significance of Jesus' Jewishness, Cone argues, is that it deals a severe blow to the christological treatments of many white theologians who conceive of the Christ-event only in universal and/or docetic terms. "Jesus' Jewishness therefore was essential to his person. He was not a 'universal' man but a particular Jew who came to fulfill God's will to liberate the oppressed. His Jewishness establishes the concreteness of his existence in history, without which Christology inevitably moves in the direction of docetism."[42] Therefore, for Cone, the Synoptic accounts of Jesus' life establish his identification with those in historical struggle for freedom revealing who they are (slaves) and what they were created to be (free human beings). When applied to the contemporary situation, "we today can lay claim on the same humanity that was liberated through Jesus' cross and resurrection. Because Jesus lived, we now know that servitude is inhuman, and that Christ has set us free to live as liberated sons and daughters of God."[43] By emphasizing Jesus' humanity in history, Cone asserts that the oppressed are empowered by the belief that the affirmation of its humanity in an oppressive society is consistent with Jesus' affirmation of humanity as a Jew in first-century Palestine and therefore is consistent with the gospel itself.

> Unless Jesus was truly like us, then we have no reason to believe that our true humanity is disclosed in his person. Without Jesus' humanity constituted in real history, we have no basis to contend that his coming bestows upon us the courage and the wisdom to struggle against injustice and oppression.[44]

Put more simply, for Cone, if the Christ-event does not permit oppressed peoples to establish a connection between it and their struggle for freedom, then first-century Palestine is irrelevant to human existence. Christologically,

[40] Cone, *A Black Theology of Liberation*, 212.
[41] Cone, *God of the Oppressed*, 119.
[42] Ibid.
[43] Ibid., 120.
[44] Ibid.

therefore, who Jesus is today is found by relating Jesus' past with his present activity. Black people affirm them both simultaneously and thus dialectically.[45]

This dialectical relationship is also found in Cone's treatment of the cross and resurrection. The former, for Cone, allows black people to connect its existence with that of Jesus. The latter, according to Cone, assures the realization of liberation through Jesus' transcending the limitations of human existence. Thus Cone contends that the resurrection reveals that divine liberation will be victorious over human oppression.

> On the one hand, through faith, black people transcended spatial and temporal existence and affirmed Jesus' past as disclosed in the historicity of his life and death on the cross.
>
> But on the other hand, black people's faith that Jesus was raised from the dead meant that his historicity and humanity are not the only relevant factors about his person. He is also the divine One who transcends the limitations of history by making himself present in our contemporary existence. When God raised Jesus from the dead, he affirmed that Jesus' historical identification with the freedom of the poor was in fact divinity taking on humanity for the purpose of liberating human beings from sin and death.[46]

This leads Cone to conclude that the resurrection is profoundly political. Since Jesus came to liberate oppressed Jews from social, economic, and political oppression, his resurrection not only frees the oppressed to struggle for its freedom but also assures its realization.

> This new knowledge about themselves and the world, as disclosed in and through the resurrection, requires that the poor practice political activity against the social and economic structure that makes them poor. Not to fight is to deny the reality of Christ's presence with us in the struggle to liberate the slaves from bondage.[47]

This new knowledge that the oppressed acquire about themselves and the world is why Cone contends that to speak of the historical Jesus alone is insufficient. The task of theology, for Cone, is not to keep Jesus confined to the first century but to relate Jesus' life to the black struggle in America, asking, "What is his relevance to the black community today?" In Cone's judgment, this means that any substantive christology must ultimately be determined not by Christ's historical value but his "soteriological value." Therefore, for Cone: "It is the oppressed community in the situation of liberation that determines the meaning and scope of Jesus Christ. We know who Jesus *was* and *is* when we encounter the brutality of oppression in his community as

---

[45] Ibid., 124.
[46] Ibid., 124–5.
[47] Ibid., 125.

it seeks to be what it is, in accordance with his resurrection."[48] According to Cone, since the black community is oppressed simply because it is black, the importance of Jesus Christ must be found in his blackness.

> If he is not black as we are, then the resurrection has little significance for our times. Indeed, if he cannot be what we are, we cannot be who he is. Our being with him is dependent on his being with us in the oppressed black condition revealing to us what is necessary for our liberation.[49]

In fact, for Cone, any christology that does not depart from Christ's blackness is a denial of the New Testament. Given that we live in a society where whiteness is depicted as good and blackness as bad, Cone contends that the black Christ comes to identify with blackness, exposing the depravity of the values of white society. Since this country has achieved its sense of moral and religious idealism by oppressing blacks, the black Christ leads the warfare against the white assault on blackness by striking at white values and white religion.[50]

While Cone recognizes that blackness as a christological title may not be applicable to every historical context, he also asserts that conceiving of Christ as exclusively universal in every context is not Christian theology. Rather, the validity of any christological title in a given context is to be measured, according to Cone, by this:

> Whether in the particularity of its time it points to God's universal will to liberate particular people from inhumanity. This is exactly what blackness does in contemporary social existence in America. If we American blacks and whites are to understand who Jesus is for us today, we must view his presence as continuous with his past and future coming which is best seen through his present blackness.[51]

This is why Cone asserts that the concept of blackness symbolizes what the world means by oppression and what the gospel means by liberation. The black Christ discloses that blackness is not what the world says it is. It further instills in blacks a revolutionary spirit by rebelling against the evil of white society and informing them that this revolutionary spirit is necessary for its empowerment. Blackness is a manifestation of the being of God in that it reveals that neither divinity nor humanity reside in white definitions but in the liberation of humanity from captivity.[52] Therefore, for Cone: "In a society that defines blackness as evil and whiteness as good, the theological significance of Jesus is found in the possibility of human liberation

[48] Cone, *A Black Theology of Liberation*, 213.
[49] Ibid.
[50] Ibid., 215.
[51] Cone, *God of the Oppressed*, 135–6.
[52] Cone, *A Black Theology of Liberation*, 216.

through blackness. Jesus is the black Christ!"[53] We are now faced with the question of where this liberation occurs—in history or beyond. The answer is found in Cone's eschatological treatment.

Eschatology

Cone's eschatological treatment departs from the assertions that (1) the revelation of God in Jesus as a liberator means that primary emphasis must be given to the present and (2) the resurrection assures the liberation of the oppressed in history. This is a necessary starting point, for Cone, given a context in which black people have been taught historically by white clergymen and theologians to forsake freedom on earth for a heavenly reward. Cone sees this as the most debilitating aspect of black religion.

> The most corrupting influence among the black churches was their adoption of the "white lie" that Christianity is primarily concerned with an other-worldly reality. White missionaries persuaded most black religious people that life on earth was insignificant because obedient servants of God could expect a "reward" in heaven after death.[54]

In particular, for Cone, blacks were made to believe that the laws of slavery and the law of God were synonymous and that being a faithful servant as a slave was consistent with being a slave for God. This lead slaves to conclude that God willed their enslavement and that eternal life was predicated on being a faithful slave. Therefore, slaves began to derive meaning and purpose in human existence devoid of a concern for earthly freedom. This lack of concern, according to Cone, is endemic to the contemporary black church as well.

> This other-worldly ethos is still very much a part of the black churches. This is not merely a problem of education among the clergy; mainly it shows that white power is so overwhelming in its domination of black people that many blacks have given up hope for change in this world. By reaching for heaven, they are saying that the odds are against them now; God must have something better in store for black people later.[55]

Cone maintains, however, that this is to distort the meaning of the gospel. By relinquishing any hope of freedom in this world, black people only sought comfort in the name of Jesus rather than empowerment through his revelation as a liberator. "Black people began to affirm that if one has 'Jesus,' it does not matter whether there is injustice, brutality, and suffering. Jesus thus becomes a magical name which gives the people a distorted hope in another life. Through identification with a name, unbearable suffering be-

---

[53] Ibid., 215.
[54] Cone, *Black Theology and Black Power*, 121.
[55] Ibid., 122.

comes bearable."[56] In contrast, Black Theology affirms that the oppressed are not to seek comfort in the name of Jesus but to see Jesus' life as the basis upon which they seek to liberate themselves in the present. Further, Black Theology affirms that the oppressed are to see the resurrection as that event which makes that liberation certain. The proper eschatological perspective must be grounded in the historical present thereby forcing the oppressed community to say No to unjust treatment because their present humiliation is inconsistent with their promised future.[57]

For Black Theology, that promised future of God as revealed in Jesus is one of the realization of freedom on earth begun by the cross and resurrection and to be consummated on his return. Thus, to speak of the future, for Cone, is not to speak of a heavenly bliss but of a future reality of black liberation that must begin to be shaped in the present by challenging an unjust order that perpetuates black oppression. If contemplation about the future distorts the present reality of injustice and reconciles the oppressed to unjust treatment committed against them, then it is unchristian and thus has nothing whatsoever to do with him who came to liberate us.[58] In short, Cone sees Christian eschatology as authentic only when the future is made the present, that is, when the future reality of liberation compels the oppressed to struggle in the present to make it a reality.

> Unless the future can become present, thereby forcing us to make changes in this world, what significance could eschatology have for black people who believe that their self-determination must become a reality *now*! White missionaries have always encouraged blacks to forget about present injustice and look forward to heavenly justice. But Black Theology says No insisting that we either put new meaning into Christian hope by relating it to our liberation or drop it altogether.[59]

For Cone, the meaning of Christian hope lies not in a hope for a future reward after death but a hope for liberation in history.

The resurrection is intimately connected to Cone's eschatological treatment. Christ is the future of God who stands in judgment upon the world and forces us to give an account of the present.[60] Cone contends that contrary to white theologians' emphasis on the end of time, Black Theology contends that the true meaning of the resurrection is to compel the oppressed to struggle to make the promised end consistent with existential reality. As long as we look at the resurrection of Christ and the expected "end,"

[56] Ibid.
[57] Cone, *A Black Theology of Liberation*, 241.
[58] Ibid.
[59] Ibid., 242.
[60] Ibid., 246.

we cannot reconcile ourselves to the things of the present that contradict his presence.[61]

This is why, for Cone, it is the task of Black Theology and Black Power to infuse black people with a restlessness concerning their oppression by asserting that something can be done about this world and that black attempts to change existential reality are consistent with the gospel. We now believe that something can be done about this world and we have resolved to die rather than deny the reality expressed in black self-determination.[62] This requires, according to Cone, a radical reinterpretation of heaven that destroys the credibility of white treatments that instill in blacks a contentment with this world; in other words, it requires a deideological analysis. "Heaven cannot mean accepting injustice of the present because we know we have a home over yonder. Home is where we have been placed now, and to believe in heaven is to refuse to accept hell on earth. This is one dimension of the future that cannot be sacrificed."[63] Black Theology is not so much concerned with the end of time as it is with existential reality in general and the continued suffering of blacks by whites in particular. Thus, Black Theology is not concerned with life after death but death during life, the death of black people by white people presently.

> Black Theology is an earthly theology! It is not concerned with the "last things" but with the "white thing." Black Theology like Black Power believes that the self-determination of black people must be emphasized at all costs, recognizing that there is only one question about the reality for blacks: What must we do about white racism?[64]

For Cone, to conceive of heaven as a future reward for earthly suffering (traditional eschatology) is not only unrealistic but irrelevant to the transformation of human suffering on earth. Thus, earthly reality has been significant only in it being the locus where one earns one's way into heaven. Black Theology, however, offers a stern challenge to this approach:

> There is no room in this perspective for an eschatology dealing with a "reward" in heaven. Black Theology has hope for this life. The appeal to the next life is a lack of hope. Such an appeal implies that absurdity has won and that one is left merely with an unrealistic gesture toward the future. Heavenly hope becomes a Platonic grasp for another reality because one cannot live meaningfully amid the suffering of this world.[65]

In Cone's judgment, a traditional eschatological treatment that makes suffering the means of entering the kingdom of heaven is a betrayal of the

---

[61] Ibid.
[62] Ibid., 247.
[63] Ibid.
[64] Cone, *Black Theology and Black Power,* 123.
[65] Ibid.

gospel. The following Matthean account is used most frequently in the traditional eschatological treatment:

> Blessed are those who are persecuted for righteousness' sake, for theirs is the kingdom of heaven.
> Blessed are you when people revile you and persecute you and utter all kinds of evil against you falsely on my account. Rejoice and be glad, for your reward is great in heaven, for in the same way [humans] persecuted the prophets who were before you (Matt 5:10-12).

But Black Theology rejects this treatment. It rejects the notion that the suffering of humans is consistent with God's will. It holds instead that black suffering is a product of the satanic nature of white culture and not the will of God. For God to come in Jesus means, for Cone, that God cannot will black oppression at the same time.

> This is the key to Black Theology. It refuses to embrace any concept of God which makes black suffering the will of God. Black people should not accept slavery, lynching, or any form of injustice as tending to good. It is not permissible to appeal to the idea that God's will is inscrutable or that the righteous sufferer will be rewarded in heaven. If God has made the world in which black people must suffer, and if [God] is a God who rules, guides and sanctifies the world, then [God] is a murderer. To be the God of black people, [God] must be against the oppression of black people.[66]

Thus, for Cone, radical obedience to God is not to be understood as a medium for a heavenly reward. Rather, Cone asserts that the reward is already given by God by granting humans the freedom to struggle for freedom on earth. God gives freedom to humans not as an individual reward but as a means of empowering the human race. In Cone's view, this is the meaning of justification by faith. For Cone, Paul was in essence saying that all human strivings for a heavenly reward were/are futile. Righteousness is not earned, it is given freely by God. Thus, according to Cone, to speak of a reward for "righteous" activity is a denial rather than an affirmation of faith. Affirmation of faith, then, comes only when humans recognize that they are incapable of achieving salvation through merit; they can only be justified by the grace of God.

> When Paul uses the term "justification" in reference to Christ he means that sinful [humanity], through complete trust alone, is accepted by God and is declared and treated as a righteous [human]. He is emphasizing [humanity's] inability to make [themselves] righteous. All human strivings are nil; [humanity] cannot earn God's acceptance (Rom 3:20-23; Gal 3:22). Salvation is by the free grace of God.[67]

---

[66] Ibid., 124–5.
[67] Ibid., 125.

Thus the righteousness of God is made manifest, argues Cone, in those humans who are currently struggling to realize the eschatological promise of God—the liberation of humanity. The truly righteous human is not seeking a reward from God, for the reward is the liberation of humanity. To seek a personal reward, in Cone's view, is to take on another form of enslavement.

> The true Christian . . . cannot be concerned about a reward in heaven. Rather he [or she] is a [person] who, through the freedom granted in Christ, is ready to plunge . . . into the evils of the world, revolting against all inhuman powers which enslave [humans]. He [or she] does not seek salvation for he [or she] knows that to seek it is to lose it. "He that would save his life will lose it. He who loses his life for my sake will gain it." He [or she] is a rebel against inhumanity and injustice.[68]

This means that though Black Theology is primarily concerned with history, it does not limit freedom to history. For to be enslaved to history is to fall prey to what the New Testament refers to as "law and death." But precisely because Black Theology sees beyond history to the eschatological future of God's liberation as exemplified in the resurrection, the efforts of whites to keep black people oppressed will fail. Thus, the resurrection allows the oppressed to transcend their existential reality of oppression to see God's eschatological future and most importantly instill in them a desire to make that future the present.

> If death is the ultimate power and life has no future beyond this world, then the rulers of the state who control the policemen and military are indeed our masters. They have our future in their hands and the oppressed can be made to obey laws of injustice. But if the oppressed, while living in history, can nonetheless see beyond it; they can visualize an eschatological future beyond the history of their humiliation, then "the *sigh* of the oppressed," to use Marx's phrase, can become a cry of revolution against the established order.[69]

Having confirmed that black liberation occurs in history, the question now becomes *how*.

Revolution and Violence

Cone's treatment of revolution and violence begins with the question, "How is Christianity related to the black revolution in America?" This question, for Cone, arises out of an American context that affirms the "discontinuity between 'blackness-revolution' and the gospel of Jesus." In America, "law and order" means obedience to the law of white people, and "stability" means the continuation of the present in the light of the past—defined and

---

[68] Ibid., 125–6.
[69] James H. Cone, "Freedom, History, and Hope," *The Journal of the Interdenominational Theological Center* 1 (Fall 1973) 64.

limited by George Washington, Abraham Lincoln, and Richard Nixon.[70] Revolution then means anything that challenges the "sacredness" of the past which is tantamount to usurping the rule of white oppressors.[71] However, according to Cone, black revolution means blacks taking control of their destiny, that is, no longer allowing whites to define their humanity or write their history. History bears Cone witness that whites will portray blacks in a manner that furthers the sociopolitical interests of the white community. Therefore, for Cone, black revolution means realizing the eschatological future of God, in other words, the liberation of black people by destroying the validity of the historical claims of white supremacy regarding the humanity of black people, destroying the meaning of white revolution—passive obedience to law and order.

> But for black people, revolution means that blacks no longer accept the history of white people as the key to their existence in the future. It also means they are prepared to do what is necessary in order to assume that their present and future existence will be defined by black visions of reality.[72]

Put another way, Cone's treatment of black revolution seeks to establish a tension between a history of white supremacy and a future of black liberation by challenging the present reality of white supremacy with the eschatological vision of the liberation of all oppressed peoples. The black revolution involves tension between the actual and the possible, the "white-past" and the "black-future," and the black community accepting the responsibility of defining the world according to its "open possibilities."[73]

Pragmatically, black revolution, for Cone, means a radical confrontation with a racist society. In so doing, Black Theology seeks to imbue blacks with a new value system that urges them to destroy white racism rather than accommodating it. Revolution is not merely a "change of heart" but a radical encounter with the structure of white racism, with the full intention of destroying its menacing power.[74]

Cone cautions, however, that revolution is not to be confused with protest. Cone explains that protest assumes change is possible within the current system through an appeal to the conscience of whites. It further assumes that the corollary to such an approach is black inclusion in the mainstream of American society. However, in Cone's opinion revolution assumes that the current system is incapable of reform and therefore seeks

---

[70] James H. Cone, "Black Theology on Revolution, Violence, and Reconciliation," *Union Seminary Quarterly Review* 31:1 (Fall 1975) 5.

[71] Ibid.

[72] Ibid.

[73] Ibid.

[74] Cone, *Black Theology and Black Power,* 136.

to usurp it with a new one. Thus, Cone asserts that the power of revolution is inescapably coercive.

In light of this, Cone sees both the pre-Civil War black church and Black Power as revolutionary. Both saw the irredeemable quality of white racism and sought its destruction by reinterpreting the thought patterns, values, and culture of black people.

> The pre-Civil War black preachers were revolutionary in that they believed that the system itself was evil and consequently urged slaves to rebel against it. The very existence of the black church meant that men like Richard Allen and Absalom Jones were convinced that the evil of racism in the white church was beyond redemption. Today the Black Power movement is an expression of this same revelatory zeal in the black community. It shuns protest and seeks to speak directly to the needs of the black community. Black Power seeks to change the structure of the black community—its thought forms, values, and culture. It tells black people to love themselves and by so doing, confront white racism with a mode of behavior inimical to everything white.[75]

Therefore, Cone sees black revolution as the creation of a new humanity that rejects white definitions of black humanity and that excludes whites from this process, given its racist history. Indeed, we blacks assume that the white position of unauthorized power as expressed in the racist character of every American institution—churches and seminaries not excluded!—renders white oppressors incapable of understanding what black humanity is, and it is thus incumbent upon us black people to become "revolutionaries of blackness," rebelling against all who enslave us.[76]

In sum, for Cone, the black revolution means a total break with the white past, "the overturning of relationships, transformation of life, and then a reconstruction," that is, a deideologizing of the white past. Theologically, this means that black people are prepared to live according to God's eschatological future as defined by the present reality of the black kingdom in the lives of oppressed peoples struggling for historical liberation.[77]

To be sure, Cone sees a correlation between black revolution and biblical theology. Both affirm, according to Cone, "the absolute sovereignty of God over [God's] creation." This means that Cone sees black people's ultimate loyalty as belonging to God. Thus, far from being only a tool for countering white supremacy, in Cone's view, revolution is a command of God in a society of unjust laws.

> The Christian . . . is obligated by a freedom grounded in the Creator to break all laws which contradict human destiny. Through disobedience to the state,

---

[75] Ibid., 137.
[76] Cone, "Black Theology on Revolution, Violence, and Reconciliation," 5.
[77] Ibid., 110.

he [or she] affirms his [or her] allegiance for God as Creator and his [or her] willingness to behave as if he [or she] believes it. Civil disobedience is a duty in a racist society.[78]

This dovetails with biblical theology's affirmation that the freedom of the human means that humanity is defined by God and not by white people. For Cone, this is the meaning of the *Imago Dei*. Thus the black refusal to permit white definitions of their humanity is not just a way of improving the condition of black people but is inextricably bound with the *Imago Dei*.

> To be for God by responding creatively to the imago Dei means that [humanity] cannot allow others to make him[/her] an It. It is this fact that makes black rebellion human and religious. When black people affirm their freedom in God, they know that they cannot obey laws of oppression. By disobeying, they not only say Yes to God but also to their own humanity and to the humanity of the white oppressor.[79]

Because, for Cone, the *Imago Dei* commands humans to rebel against efforts to reduce them to a non-human status, black revolution in a racist society is God's revolution as well.

This leads to the issue of violence and Black Theology's response to the assertion of whites that violence is a negation of the gospel of Jesus. Cone is concerned that white preoccupation with violence invariably applies to the violence of blacks and not white violence committed on black people. In so doing, Cone recognizes the ideological implications of white violence insofar as whites attempt to justify it by arguing that it is necessary for maintaining a "peaceful" society. "White people are not really concerned about violence in all cases but only when they are the victims. As long as blacks are beaten and shot, they are strangely silent, as if they are unaware of the inhumanity committed against the black community."[80] Cone sees white support of government violence on blacks in the name of "law and order" as the epitome of hypocrisy. Whites seem, according to Cone, to have the ability to recognize the violence of oppressed peoples in striking a blow for their freedom but not the violence of the state that creates and maintains oppressive contexts. Why didn't we hear from the so-called nonviolent Christians when blacks were *violently* enslaved, *violently* lynched, and *violently* ghettoized in the name of freedom and democracy?[81] Thus, for Cone:

> When whites ask me, "Are you for violence?" my rejoinder is: "Whose violence? Richard Nixon's or his victims'? The Mississippi State Police or the students at Jackson State? The Chicago Police or Fred Hampton? What the hell

[78] Cone, *Black Theology and Black Power*, 137.
[79] Ibid., 137–8.
[80] Cone, *God of the Oppressed*, 195–6.
[81] Ibid., 196.

are you talking about?" If we are going to raise the question of violence, it ought to be placed in its proper perspective.[82]

That proper perspective, in Cone's judgment, can be summarized in three points. First, violence is not only the present activity of black people in its attempt to live in a more just society but the past activity of whites in creating a society of white privilege and what they do to maintain it.

> Violence in America did not begin with the black power movement or with the Black Panther Party. Contrary to popular white opinion, violence has a long history in America. This country was born in violent revolution (remember 1776?), and it has been sustained by the violent extermination of red people and the violent enslavement of black people. This is what Rap Brown had in mind when he said that "Violence is American as cherry pie."[83]

Thus, for Cone, white thinking concerning violence is distorted insofar as it assumes that violence is only breaking societal laws. I contend, therefore, that the problem of violence is not the problem of a few black revolutionaries but the problem of a whole social structure which outwardly appears to be ordered and respectable but inwardly is "ridden by psychopathic obsessions and delusions"—racism and hatred.[84]

Second, if Black Power means the right of black people to seek its liberation by whatever means black people deem necessary, then only they have a right to say what is appropriate violence and what is not. This means that assertions regarding the state as being ordained of God and that therefore its harshest acts are more appropriate than the individual violent act or the violence of mass uprisings are unacceptable for Black Theology. This distinction is false and merely expresses an identification with the structures of power rather than with the victims of power.[85]

Third, the question, "Is the gospel of Jesus compatible with violence?" must be answered not only in the light of what Jesus did but what Jesus is doing. Thus, the task of theology, for Cone, is not simply to relate what Jesus did in first-century Palestine, but to examine what he did in the past as a basis for what he would do today. In Cone's view, Jesus' being nonviolent in the past does not mean that he would be nonviolent today. The political demographics and social context of Palestine are much different from today's demographics and therefore offer no conclusive evidence that Jesus would be nonviolent today. Therefore, Cone sees the use of the Jesus of history as an "absolute ethical guide" for his (and our) actions today as extremely suspect. According to Cone, "the gospel means liberation; and one

---

[82] Cone, "Black Theology on Revolution, Violence, and Reconciliation," 10.
[83] Cone, *God of the Oppressed,* 217–8.
[84] Ibid., 218.
[85] Ibid., 219.

essential element of that liberation is the existential burden of making decisions about human liberation without being completely sure what Jesus did or would do."[86] Therefore, Christians are not commanded, Cone contends, to adhere to a strict code of ethical principles but "to discover the will of God in a troubled and dehumanized world."

> Concretely, we must decide not between good and evil or right and wrong, but between the oppressors and the oppressed, whiteness and blackness. We must ask and answer the question, "Whose actions are consistent with God's work in history?" Either we believe that God's will is revealed in the status quo of America or in the actions of those who seek to change it.[87]

Conclusion

We began the chapter by examining Cone's "new hermeneutic" (blackness as the symbol of oppression and of the certainty of liberation). We also examined Cone's assertion that Christian theology cannot be relevant unless its doctrines are treated such that they are directly related to the emancipation of black people in America. We then applied this new hermeneutic to five of Cone's doctrines. In regard to God, Cone argues that because blackness is what the world means by oppression, God becomes black for the purpose of usurping black (human) oppression with black (divine) liberation. Concerning humanity, Cone contends that God's becoming black means humanity accepting blackness as the only way of being in the world, that is, identifying with and participating in the liberation struggle of black people. Not to do so, for Cone, is to be in sin (defining one's existence according to white standards). Further, Cone argues that only the oppressed are truly free inasmuch as they have been the recipients of white racism, on the one hand, but of God's liberating activity, on the other. Christologically, Black Theology argues that since Jesus identifies with the victims of injustice in the Bible and since those victims in this context are black, the Jesus of the Bible is the Jesus of the black experience. Eschatologically, Black Theology deideologizes the "white lie" that Christianity is an otherworldly religion and instead asserts that God's eschatological promise is one of sociopolitical liberation to be realized in history. Finally, we saw that revolution means the realization of God's liberation by deideologizing white claims concerning black humanity and that violence must be determined by the *victims* of power rather than the *structures* of power.

Because Cone was able to construct a new hermeneutic that deideologizes the ideology of white supremacy and uses that new hermeneutic as a way of reinterpreting theology for the purpose of black liberation, he passes the fourth stage of Segundo's hermeneutic circle and therefore completes it.

---

[86] Ibid.

[87] Cone, "Black Theology on Revolution, Violence, and Reconciliation," 12.

CHAPTER 5

The Case for Indigenous Deideologization

Having shown that Cone's theological method is in a process of deideologization and thus brings liberative potential to faith, I would like to conclude with a constructive piece employing the methods of both Cone and Segundo. Though the weaknesses of their theological perspectives have been well documented,[1] they complement one another regarding the unmasking

---

[1] In terms of the weaknesses of Cone's theology regarding his lack of the use of sources grounded in the black experience, see Cecil W. Cone, *Identity Crisis in Black Theology* (Nashville: African Methodist Episcopal Church, 1975); Gayraud S. Wilmore, *Black Religion and Black Radicalism*, 2nd ed., rev. and enl. (Maryknoll, N.Y.: Orbis Books, 1983); and Charles H. Long, "Structural Similarities and Dissimilarities in Black and African Theologies," *Journal of Religious Thought* 32:2 (Fall–Winter 1975). Regarding Cone's inability to develop a liberation ethic that includes reconciliation, see J. Deotis Roberts, *Liberation and Reconciliation: A Black Theology* (Philadelphia: Westminster Press, 1971). Regarding Cone's lack of grounding in black women's unique experience of oppression in America, see Delores S. Williams, *Sisters in the Wilderness: The Challenge of Womanist God-Talk* (Maryknoll, N.Y.: Orbis Books, 1993); Jacquelyn Grant, "Black Theology and the Black Woman," *Black Theology: A Documentary History, 1966–1979,* ed. Gayraud S. Wilmore and James H. Cone (Maryknoll, N.Y.: Orbis Books, 1979) 418–33. In terms of Cone's treatment of God and the question of theodicy, see William R. Jones, *Is God a White Racist?* 2nd ed. (Boston: Beacon Press, 1998). For Cone's assessment of Black Theology and its weaknesses, see the preface to the 1986 edition of *A Black Theology of Liberation.* See also *Union Seminary Quarterly Review* 31:1 (Fall 1975) for Cone's essay "Black Theology on Revolution, Violence, and Reconciliation," and critiques of it by C. Eric Lincoln, Herbert O. Edwards, Frederick Herzog, Paul Lehmann, and Helmut Gollwitzer. For critiques of Cone's theology by white theologians, see *Black Theology: A Documentary History, 1966–1979.* Regarding weaknesses in Segundo's hermeneutic circle, see Joe Holland and Peter Henriot, *Social Analysis: Linking Faith and Justice* (Maryknoll, N.Y.: Orbis Books, 1985); J. Deotis Roberts, "The Hermeneutic Circle of Black Theology," *Black Theology Today* (New York: E. Mellen Press, 1983) 3–33; and Elizabeth Schüssler Fiorenza, *Bread Not Stone: The Challenge of Feminist Biblical Interpretation* (Boston: Beacon Press, 1984). I will be saying more about Roberts' and Schüssler Fiorenza's critiques later.

of what Segundo refers to as *religio-political ideologies* in theological reflection. By religio-political ideologies Segundo means those religious assertions that seek to mask the true nature of oppressor-oppressed relationships in the name of God.[2] It is the theology of Cone that I think effectively addresses the virulent affects of religio-political ideologies in a particular context (namely the black-white relationship in America) while Segundo seeks a delegitimation of religio-political ideologies in more universal terms. That is to say, Segundo picks up where Cone leaves off in not only making religio-political ideologies an inescapable point of departure for relevant theological reflection, but also for concluding that the destruction of these ideologies through the process of deideologization is essential for liberating the oppressed. Thus, I offer a theological method that can be best described as a synthesis of the methods of Cone and Segundo that takes into account Cone's attempt to expose the religio-political ideologies in his context of America and Segundo's method for exposing those ideologies, in other words, the hermeneutic circle, in which he encourages liberation theologians to apply to their respective contexts. I refer to this theological method as *indigenous deideologization*. I proceed in this final chapter by first looking at Cone's treatment of ideologies and then turning to Segundo's theology and some of the ideological factors in theological reflection itself he found problematic, thus calling into existence the need for a hermeneutic circle. Last, I formally treat the notion of indigenous deideologization.

Cone's Theology of Liberation

Cone's theological perspective can be best described as the attempt to maintain a dialectical relationship between biblical revelation and social existence. In particular, Cone is interested in showing that the biblical revelation of God in Jesus Christ is one of sociopolitical liberation for the oppressed and that for our social existence this means the liberation of black people from white supremacy. Further, Cone maintains that this liberation occurs in history and is not ethereal. In so doing, Cone seeks to challenge long-standing religious assertions by white clergymen and religious leaders that black freedom comes after death and only after having served whites well on earth. For Cone, if God revealed Godself in Jesus in history, then the fulfillment of the promises of God as revealed in Scripture must also occur in history. According to Cone:

> In the Bible, revelation and history are inseparable from history and faith. History is the arena in which God's revelation takes place. Unlike many non-Christian religions, the God of the Bible makes the divine will and purpose

[2] See Juan Luis Segundo, *Faith and Ideologies*, trans. John Drury (Maryknoll, N.Y.: Orbis Books, 1984). See also *The Historical Jesus of the Synoptics*, trans. John Drury (Maryknoll, N.Y.: Orbis Books, 1985).

known through participation in human history. That is why Christianity has been described as a historical religion. It is a religion which affirms that we know who God is by what God does in human history. In fact, there is no revelation of God without history. The two are inseparable.[3]

Thus given white supremacist claims about black liberation being ethereal in nature, establishing the revelation of God in history as one of black liberation is crucial for Black Theology. As such, Cone wants to conceive of the dialectical relationship between biblical revelation and social existence such that it effectively refutes white supremacist claims that God's revelation is ahistorical and/or that black strivings for freedom do not have divine significance. Cone instead seeks to establish that the dialectical relationship between biblical revelation and social existence means that God came to set at liberty those who are oppressed. Since in the twentieth century that oppressed people is black people, then a theological perspective rooted in blackness (the basis of black oppression) and its liberation is the most relevant theological expression of our time. In so doing, a Black Theology of liberation becomes the theological perspective that most clearly reveals the link between biblical revelation and social context.

Making blackness his point of departure demonstrates that Cone undertook a process I consider to be essential for any relevant theology—apply a pervading ideological suspicion to the theological terrain seeking to identify and destroy the credibility of those religious assertions that sought/seek to legitimate black oppression. That is to say, his theology had to be in a process of deideologization. In the previous chapters my intent was to show that this ideological suspicion is clearly present in Cone's theology and further that it is possessed of deideological dimensions. Further, while these deideological dimensions are found throughout Cone's major works, he devotes a chapter to ideologies and their significance in theological reflection in what I consider his most mature work, *God of the Oppressed.*

Cone proceeds to examine ideologies in the context of Black Theology by raising the question: How do we distinguish our words about God from God's Word, our wishes from God's will, our dreams and aspirations from the work of God's Spirit?[4] Cone sees this as a critical issue not only for Black Theology but Christian theology in general. However, for the purposes of Black Theology, Cone is interested in effectively refuting the claims of white theology that Black Theology is nothing more than an ideological ruse for promoting black politics. Cone responds to the claims of white theologians about Black Theology once again by examining the relationship between

---

[3] James H. Cone, *A Black Theology of Liberation,* Twentieth Anniversary Edition (Maryknoll, N.Y.: Orbis Books, 1990) 46.

[4] James H. Cone, *God of the Oppresse*d (San Francisco: Harper & Row, 1975) 84.

biblical revelation and social existence. He argues that, because "in one word, God's revelation means *liberation*—nothing more, nothing less," the efforts of blacks to free themselves from white supremacy is not only synonymous with God's will but is God's will. Thus, for Cone, blacks are not using revelation to promote a purely political agenda but are instead a contemporary manifestation of that revelation. Therefore, any claim that Black Theology is nothing more than black politics, in Cone's judgment, must be established in light of Jesus' proclamation that he came to liberate those who are oppressed. Unless we black theologians can make an adequate distinction between divine revelation and human aspirations, there is nothing to keep Black Theology from identifying God's will with anything black people should decide to do at any given historical moment.[5] Moreover, valid theology is distinguished from heresy only if the former is bound to the divine One who is the ground of its existence.[6] According to Cone, this means that theology becomes ideology when the dialectical relationship between fidelity to the gospel and contemporary reality betrays Jesus' understanding of himself as a liberator of the oppressed. In Cone's view, this is what white supremacists have made theology—a medium for justifying the status quo by conceiving of God's revelation as one that condones oppression.

Cone then proceeds to analyze the distinction between God's revelation and human aspirations using H. Richard Niebuhr's *Christ and Culture*. After explaining the five typologies Niebuhr sets forth regarding the Christ-culture relationship in Christian history, Cone expresses his concern with Niebuhr's definitions of Christ and culture. While Cone agrees with Niebuhr's claim that culture informs yet also limits the theologian's understanding of Christ, he is troubled by Niebuhr's inability to make the relationship between revelation and the liberation of oppressed peoples his christological starting point. If we are to accept the biblical revelation as the point of departure for a picture of Christ, then we must ask whether it is possible to talk about Christ in any sense without making his identity with the oppressed the starting point.[7] Cone finds similar problems with Niebuhr's definition of culture. Like his description of Christ, his definition of culture is inadequate in terms of its lack of specificity in relation to the oppressor and oppressed, whites and blacks.[8] Cone's conclusion is that by not engaging in more specificity concerning oppressor-oppressed contexts, Niebuhr simply highlights the complexity of the Christ-culture relationship but does not treat it in such a way that he prevents the construction of a "valid" theology that emerges out of white culture—a culture that has meant the en-

---

[5] Ibid., 84–5.
[6] Ibid., 88.
[7] Ibid., 89.
[8] Ibid., 90.

slavement and exploitation of black people and is diametrically opposed to the will of God. In other words, Cone sees in Niebuhr's treatment a dangerous universalism that does not address the concreteness of human pain and suffering and, in so doing, allows for both black and white culture to be affirmed as the continuing work of Christ. For example, if the biblical Christ is the liberator of the oppressed from the sociopolitical bondage inflicted by the oppressors, then can it be said that Jesus Christ relates to both cultural expressions in the same way?[9] Cone categorically rejects any Christ-culture treatment that allows for a relationship between Jesus Christ and white culture. Cone opts instead for a Christ-culture relationship that affirms the biblical witness that Christ comes as a liberator of the oppressed, thus making the culture of the oppressed and its strivings for freedom a twentieth-century expression of the biblical witness. In this sense, Cone has maintained the dialectical relationship between biblical revelation and social existence rooted in the liberation of the oppressed.

Cone further examines ideologies using Mannheim's *Ideology and Utopia.* Cone understands ideologies to be "deformed thought, meaning that a certain idea or ideas are nothing but the function of subjective intent of an individual or group. Truth therefore becomes what an individual wishes it to be as defined in accordance with a person's subjective desires."[10] For Cone, that deformed thought in this context is white supremacy passing off as truth the notion that God favors a white superiority–black inferiority relationship for the perpetuation of white privilege at the expense of black dehumanization.

In particular Cone seeks to contextualize Mannheim's notion of *particular ideologies* and *total ideologies.* According to Mannheim, wherein particular ideologies occur in the psychological realm, total ideologies occur in the sociological realm and thus the overall worldview of the person. Black Theology contextualizes these categories by maintaining that ideologies in the particular sense is the development of a biblical hermeneutical approach that perpetuates the interests of the privilege. It is the interpretation of Scripture as if the poor and their liberation is incidental to the gospel message. Such an approach, in Cone's view, potentially lead to two dangerous consequences for the oppressed. First, particular ideologies have had a tendency historically to produce in the oppressed a static quietism and passivity that hinder liberation efforts. It creates in the oppressed, for Cone, a complacency that frowns on or devalues black leadership models of strong resistance to white supremacy. Second, in Cone's opinion particular ideologies, especially in the American context, compel "successful" members of the oppressed to assume that striving for freedom is no longer a neces-

---

[9] Ibid.
[10] Ibid., 91.

sary endeavor to be undertaken, citing their success as proof that strong resistance to white supremacy should be reconsidered. This ultimately leads, for Cone, to the attenuating of black efforts for liberation.

Ideology in the total sense "represents that form of thinking whose intellectual grid excludes a priori the truth of the biblical story." Cone has in mind mostly intellectuals who treat God, Christ, and other aspects of the faith as if they have no relation to oppressed strivings for freedom and/or that the biblical message is exclusively one of spiritual endowment that divorces God's revelation in Christ from the poor and their freedom. Rather than a truth rooted in God's revelation as being one of liberation, for Cone "truth is often interpreted in legalistic and philosophical categories. Its content is usually information about God to be known either through assent to doctrine as exegeted by scholars or through rational and philosophical discourse."[11] Thus, Cone sees in the theological and philosophical treatments of many scholars in the white community minimal effort in relating biblical revelation with social existence such that the former is made relevant to the latter by affirming oppressed struggles for freedom as the will of God. In so doing, Cone does not see any danger in white theologians and philosophers taking sides—indeed the biblical witness demands it! What Cone struggles with is the side that they have historically taken—the side of the rich and powerful. In view of the distinction between ideology and social a priori and our contention that divine truth is God's liberation of the weak from oppression, the question that theologians must ask is not whether their theologies are determined by social interests, but whose social interests determine their theologies: the oppressed or the oppressors?[12] Therefore, theology that does not emerge from the historical consciousness of the poor is ideology.[13]

Finally, Cone examines ideologies within the context of story. While Cone concedes that all groups of people have stories unique to their culture or race, he also maintains that the ideological nature of story must be critiqued on two fronts. First, Cone contends that story must not remain enclosed in one's own community. Rather, one should be able to move out of one's own story and into another way of viewing story. Viewing the world only through one's own story leads to highly parochial worldviews that ultimately breed superior thinking about one's own context. Thus, parochialism should never be a basis for understanding story. This leads to Cone's second concern: if parochial worldviews breed superior thinking, then theologians and religionists will invariably tend to codify them into religious dogmas which in turn engender superior or ideological thinking in that particular

[11] Ibid., 94.
[12] Ibid., 95.
[13] Ibid., 96.

community religiously. According to Cone: "When people can no longer listen to other people's stories, they become enclosed within their own social context, treating their distorted visions of reality as the whole truth. And then they feel that they must destroy other stories, which bear witness that life can be lived in another way."[14] This, for Cone, is what has happened in the black-white context in America. He sees white people's enslavement of blacks and the extermination of Native Americans as an attempt to deprive both of their stories in the attempt to establish white culture not only as the best story, but the only story. Cone sees this as the essence of ideologies.

> White people were saying that black and red stories were lies and superstitions that have no place in a "civilized" country. From some perspectives, the white story of black enslavement may be a "valid" story, but from the perspective of the victims, it is a tale of terror and bloodshed. From the biblical point of view it is an epic of rebellion, the usurpation of God's rule. In other words, it is ideology.[15]

Cone instead argues that if we are the Christians we claim to be, then we must bring our respective stories before the bar of the biblical story to see if our stories are in sync with biblical revelation. More importantly, for our purposes, Cone maintains that we must take our stories beyond the biblical story to Christian tradition (Luther, Calvin, Zwingli, etc.), the black Christian tradition (David Walker, Harriet Tubman, Frederick Douglass, Martin Luther King Jr., etc.), personal testimonies both in and out of the Church, animal tales (Br'er Fox), black music (blues, spirituals, and rap),[16] slave narratives,[17] indigenous religions,[18] non-Christian religions, and the indige-

---

[14] Ibid., 103.

[15] Ibid.

[16] See James H. Cone, *The Spirituals and the Blues* (New York: Seabury Press, 1972). See also Anthony Pinn, *Why Lord? Suffering and Evil in Black Theology* (New York: Continuum, 1995). See especially Pinn's construction of what he refers to as nitty-gritty hermeneutics. Although Pinn is primarily concerned with the question of theodicy in this work, he lifts up the possibilities of substantive black dialogue about the nature of God existing outside traditional ecclesial thinking, namely in blues, rap, and humanist thought.

[17] While Cone dealt to a reasonable degree with slave narratives, there has emerged a "second generation" of black theologians who have treated them extensively in the development of their theological perspectives. See Dwight N. Hopkins and George C. L. Cummings, eds., *Cut Loose Your Stammering Tongue: Black Theology in the Slave Narratives* (Maryknoll, N.Y.: Orbis Books, 1991). See also Dwight Hopkins, *Shoes that Fit Our Feet: Sources for a Constructive Black Theology* (Maryknoll, N.Y.: Orbis Books, 1993); Dwight Hopkins, *Down, Up, and Over: Slave Religion and Black Theology* (Minneapolis: Fortress Press, 2000).

[18] This is an area of the development of Black Theology that can go a long way in uncovering the liberating elements in black religion particularly as it relates to

nous voices of oppressed peoples in Africa, Asia, and Latin America, given that oppression extends beyond the American context. Hence, theological reflection is most productive, for Cone, when it employs both the tools of formal theology *and the voices of indigenous peoples.* It is here that social existence most closely dovetails with biblical revelation.

Although Cone demonstrates that his theological perspective is rooted in a pervading ideological suspicion concerning religio-political ideologies and their effect on black freedom both in the academy and the society, as well as makes the voices of indigenous peoples a source for theological reflection, he did not make ideologies and deideologization his theological point of departure. He did not depart from the presupposition that if theology is to be a viable source for the liberation of the oppressed, theology must first liberate itself from its ideological ties with the status quo. For that, we must examine the theology of Juan Luis Segundo.

Segundo's Liberation of Theology

Like Cone, Segundo is concerned with the dialectical relationship between biblical revelation and social existence, a relationship Segundo refers to in more simple terms: "to combine the disciplines that open up the past with the disciplines that help to explain the present." Unlike Cone, whose understanding of this relationship departs from the black-white relationship in America, Segundo begins with academic theology and its uncritical acceptance of a Church tradition that seeks to apply one interpretation of Scripture to constantly changing historical contexts. Segundo wonders whether this ahistorical hermeneutical approach is not only able to explain the present but whether it is able to transform the present, particularly oppressor-oppressed contexts. Segundo understands this approach on the part of the Church and academic theology not to be accidental but part of a larger "superstructure" that seeks to maintain the status quo. Thus, for Segundo, one must apply a thorough ideological suspicion to traditional ways of interpreting Scripture given that they have, for the most part, brought legitimacy to a larger ideological superstructure that sanctions the worldview of dominant classes. This is why, for Segundo, the liberation theologian must not begin with the application of a given interpretation of Scripture to any and all historical contexts. Rather, the liberation theologian must reverse the process and begin with the historical context and then move to divine revelation given that "anything and everything involving ideas, including theology, is intimately bound up with the existing social order in at least an

---

debunking historical claims regarding their so-called primitive and superstitious natures. On this aspect of Black Theology see Will Coleman, *Tribal Talk: Black Theology, Hermeneutics, and African/American Ways of "Telling the Story"* (University Park: Pennsylvania State University Press, 2000).

unconscious way." Only by beginning with history and then divine revelation, for Segundo, will we be able to connect the biblical past in a liberating way to the present. If not, Segundo fears that the language of liberation will eventually be incorporated into the "deeper mechanisms of oppression," which includes theology. Therefore, what is needed, according to Segundo, is the construction of a theological method that is both flexible enough to change with constantly changing historical contexts, yet rigid enough to prevent the language of liberation from being diluted by those of dominant classes. What is needed, for Segundo, is a theological method capable of liberating theology from itself and its duplicitous collaboration with the Church. Segundo refers to this method as *the hermeneutic circle*.

Segundo's concern for meshing the present with the past is clearly seen in his definition of the hermeneutic circle. As stated in the Introduction, Segundo defines it as

> the continuing change in our interpretation of the Bible which is dictated by the continuing change in our present-day needs, both individual and societal. . . . And the circular nature of this interpretation stems from the fact that each new reality obliges us to interpret the Word of God afresh, to change reality accordingly, and then go back and reinterpret the Word of God again, and so on.

By structuring the definition of the hermeneutic circle in this way, Segundo is seeking to challenge the traditional mode of scriptural interpretation by the Church and academic theology that make faith and revelation dogmas of Church tradition that are not historically and culturally conditioned. In such an approach, Segundo argues that theology's response to contemporary problems will be inadequate at best insofar as it will be ensnared in an obsolete, conservative Weltanschaaung. But more importantly, for Segundo, such an approach will fail to see, let alone address, theology and the Church's role in creating and perpetuating religio-political ideologies and what can be done to destroy their influence. Hence, the hermeneutic circle is constructed in the attempt to root theological reflection not only in exposing religio-political ideologies, but also in the construction of theological assertions rooted in sociopolitical liberation; in other words, to put theological reflection in a process of deideologization. Only then, for Segundo, will theology be capable of liberating oppressed peoples.

As it relates to this work, Segundo does not want the hermeneutic circle relegated to Latin America. He encourages theologians in their respective contexts to employ the hermeneutic circle (or a similar version) as a means of theologizing out of the particular historical and cultural conditions unique to their setting. Thus, I have tried to show in this work that Cone, although he did not use the hermeneutic circle in his theology, is a representative example of how the process of deideologization is achieved in the

United States. Cone's theology effectively addresses the dialectical relationship of the past and the present, providing theology with some "here-and-now criteria," making the transformation of the black-white relationship in America the historical and cultural problem that Christian theology must liberatively respond to if its relevance is to be maintained. Cone's ideological suspicion and his integration of biblical revelation and social existence are apparent throughout his works, and his treatment of liberation is such that it would be very difficult to incorporate it into the status quo. As such, his theology is in a process of deideologization.

Yet, if Segundo encourages liberation theologians to apply the hermeneutic circle to their contexts, if it is to be ultimately viable in the black-white context in the United States, it will need to be amended on two fronts.

J. Deotis Roberts, in his article "The Hermeneutic Circle of Black Theology,"[19] argues that Segundo's hermeneutic circle does not meet the needs of Black Theology in two ways. First, Roberts maintains that Segundo's notion of liberation is not holistic enough. That is, while Segundo lifts up sociopolitical liberation, Roberts is concerned that he does not expand that understanding of liberation to the "healing" dimension of faith, that is, it does not include what Roberts refers to as "persons-in-community." Second, although for Roberts Segundo's hermeneutic circle focuses on biblical texts (which is important for him), there is no provision for the rich oral tradition of African culture; thus, it fails to establish the link between the African past and the African American present. Roberts puts it this way:

> [The hermeneutic circle's] focus is upon biblical texts but it does not allow for a rich oral tradition. Segundo's circle would place an undue restriction on the dialogue between African and black theologians. This dialogue has already reached into the Caribbean and will surely involve people of African descent in Latin America.[20]

While I am not altogether in agreement with Roberts' conclusions, his critique of Segundo's hermeneutic circle and its implications for a viable Black Theology warrants serious consideration. While liberation theology understands itself to be a corrective theology bringing a balance of sociopolitical liberation to spiritual liberation, it must not totally disregard the latter. To be sure, liberation theology must continue to give more prominence to sociopolitical liberation given the horrendous effects of sociopolitical oppression on the lives of oppressed peoples. Yet it must also be mindful that there is an inner liberation of the human subject that drives that subject onward to a more meaningful personal relationship with God and *subsequently on*

---

[19] This article is found among many other insightful articles by Roberts in his *Black Theology Today*, 3–33.

[20] Ibid., 7.

to a life of struggle and sacrifice against unjust powers (this corollary of one's personal relationship with God must continue to be emphasized more by both the academy and the Church).

More importantly, for our purposes, Roberts' identification of Segundo's emphasis on biblical texts but not oral tradition exposes a serious weakness in the hermeneutic circle. In general, most oppressed peoples have a strong oral tradition, and the failure to tap into this reservoir particularly as it relates to refuting the degenerative historical depictions of oppressed peoples by their colonizers would rob liberation theologies of much of their liberative potential. In particular, indigenous deideologization would suffer greatly and lose its vitality if there were no meaningful dialogues between native peoples and those in diasporas. If indigenous voices are stifled by theological method (regardless of its intentions to do otherwise) that method would become a religio-political ideology rather than a liberative response to it. As such, strategies for liberation in any context where indigenous voices are not included would prove to be misguided.

Second, Elisabeth Schüssler Fiorenza also has a concern regarding Segundo's hermeneutic circle. In her book *Bread Not Stone: The Challenge of Feminist Biblical Interpretation*,[21] she argues that although the hermeneutic circle calls for a reinterpretation of Scripture in light of the struggle of the oppressed for liberation, Segundo did not go far enough with his analysis. According to Schüssler Fiorenza, Segundo fails to see beyond the Bible to the repressive nature of biblical traditions themselves in the formulation of both Old and New Testament canons. Put another way, Schüssler Fiorenza is concerned that the ideological suspicion that Segundo implores the oppressed to apply to its existential reality is not applied by Segundo himself to scriptural traditions. Though Schüssler Fiorenza concedes that Segundo is not seeking to establish that meaning and liberation are found in the content of Scripture but in the process of deutro-learning,[22] she also understands Segundo to be derelict in not recognizing biblical tradition as an area of critical analysis. In so doing, he is engaging more in a "hermeneutics of consent" rather than a "hermeneutics of suspicion." In comparing and contrasting Segundo's thought with neo-orthodox theology, Schüssler Fiorenza explains:

---

[21] Boston: Beacon Press, 1984.

[22] Segundo maintains that we come to learn Christian faith not from God or the Bible but from people in our communities who have, in turn, learned the faith from someone else who teaches us about God and the Bible. Segundo refers to the people who teach us the faith as "referential witnesses." But, more importantly, Segundo argues that because we not only learn the faith from a referential witness but also learn the process of increasing our knowledge of the faith from someone else, he refers to this process as deutro-learning. See his *Faith and Ideologies*, 71ff.

[Segundo] shares with neo-orthodoxy the hermeneutical presupposition that scriptural traditions are meaningful and that they can therefore claim our obedience and demand a "hermeneutics of consent." In contrast to neo-orthodox theology, Segundo does not claim that meaning and liberation are found in the *content* of Scripture but rather in the process of learning how to learn.[23]

Schüssler Fiorenza's conclusion is that Segundo does not accomplish what he sets out to do. When considering that Segundo's project is devoted to the development of a theological method such that the language of liberation cannot be absorbed by the status quo and is robbed of its true content, Schüssler Fiorenza contends that a hermeneutics of consent and deutro-learning do not realize this insofar as both can still be distorted. The former, for Schüssler Fiorenza, does not allow for a critical evaluation of the ideological nature of biblical traditions, thereby lending tacit approval to the patriarchal customs of biblical history. The latter can be distorted, according to Schüssler Fiorenza, in that given the uncritical evaluation of biblical traditions, the prospects of a hermeneutical learning process not being intertwined with the methodological consent to patriarchal biblical traditions are dismal. Segundo must, therefore, either demonstrate that this is not the case or formalize this learning process so that the advocacy stance[24] becomes an abstract principle not applicable to the contents of the Bible.[25] In short, according to Schüssler Fiorenza, a hermeneutics of consent and deutro-learning are defective tools in the construction of a liberation hermeneutic insofar as they do not allow for critical engagement by the liberation theologian of either the biblical texts or biblical hermeneutical methodologies.

> Such a proposal . . . does not allow us to judge whether a text or interpretation is appropriate and helpful to the struggle of the oppressed for liberation. The failure to bring a critical evaluation to bear upon the biblical texts and upon the process of interpretation within Scripture and tradition is one reason liberation theologians' use of the Bible often approximates that of scholars who seek texts as proof of their positions. To avoid this, liberation

[23] Ibid., 51.

[24] The advocacy stance is a concept of liberation theologians that maintains that all theological reflection, be it explicit or implicit, advocates a stance for or against oppressed peoples. It further asserts that theology is incapable of engaging in intellectual objectivity in a world wrought with global racial and gender hegemony. In this case, Schüssler Fiorenza holds that Segundo's application of the advocacy stance to the contents of the Bible with a hermeneutics of suspicion is a methodological Russian roulette given the oppressive character of some biblical narratives. Therefore, Schüssler Fiorenza sees Segundo as being far better served not applying the advocacy stance to the contents of the Bible.

[25] Schüssler Fiorenza, *Bread Not Stone,* 51–2.

hermeneutics must reflect on the fact that the process of interpretation of Scripture is not necessarily liberative.[26]

Thus what is needed, in Schüssler Fiorenza's view, is a biblical hermeneutical methodology that holds up the sacred nature of the Bible while at the same time not precluding a critical evaluation of it and the traditions that shaped its compilation.

Schüssler Fiorenza has provided us with valuable insights for amending the hermeneutic circle. Her recognition that Segundo does not engage in a critique of the biblical traditions that shaped the Old and New Testament canons does not send us forward to the present and oppressor-oppressed contexts, but backward to the historical and cultural conditions and particularly to the patriarchal traditions that influenced the way the Bible redactors structured biblical texts. As such, the exegetical suspicion that the third stage of the hermeneutic circle calls for must not only be applied to biblical hermeneutical approaches that have given divine sanction to current oppressor-oppressed contexts, but also to the deeply entrenched patriarchal customs of biblical times that have made their way into the Bible. Only then will Segundo's "hermeneutics of consent" become a thoroughgoing "hermeneutics of suspicion." More importantly, by minimizing the entry of patriarchal traditions into biblical hermeneutical approaches, it also decreases the possibility of "learning how to learn" from someone who expresses his/her faith in repressive ways.[27]

Hence with Cone's attempt to use Christian theology as a means of black liberation and Segundo's efforts to liberate theology from itself, we have the basis of a viable theological method, amendments included, that addresses both the particular (Cone) and the universal (Segundo) dimensions necessary for substantive theological reflection. With this foundation as an appropriate backdrop, I now seek to make the case for indigenous deideologization.

---

[26] Ibid., 52.

[27] While there are other critiques concerning Segundo's theology in general, these two works (along with Holland and Henriot) are the most widely-known critiques of Segundo's hermeneutic circle which is my concern in this work. For other treatments of Segundo's theology see Roger Haight, *An Alternative Vision: An Interpretation of Liberation Theology* (New York: Paulist Press, 1985); Alfred T. Hennelley, *Theologies in Conflict: The Challenge of Juan Luis Segundo* (Maryknoll, N.Y.: Orbis Books, 1979); Arthur F. McGovern, *Liberation Theology and Its Critics: Toward an Assessment* (Maryknoll, N.Y.: Orbis Books, 1979); Frances Stefano, *The Absolute Value of Human Action in the Theology of Juan Luis Segundo* (Lanham, Md.: University Press of America, 1992); Anthony J. Tambasco, *The Bible for Ethics: Juan Luis Segundo and First World Ethics* (Lanham, Md.: University Press of America, 1981).

The Case for Indigenous Deideologization

Having examined the theological methods of both Cone and Segundo, my objective is to now incorporate them into a constructive theological method that I have chosen to call *indigenous deideologization.* It is a theological method that strives for a third way between Cone's perspective and his concentration on the black-white encounter in America and Segundo's perspective and the hermeneutic circle that lifts up the significance of religio-political ideologies in theological reflection and their need to be deideologized if theology is to first liberate itself and then play a significant role in bringing about sociopolitical liberation for oppressed peoples.

Thus, indigenous deideologization brings together the tools of formal academic theology and the voices of indigenous peoples in the attempt to codify and document the voices and contributions of those who have been written out of history—the voices of those of "the underside of history." But because indigenous deideologization sees challenging the credibility of religio-political ideologies that legitimate the dominance of one group over another as the necessary starting point for the theologian, it is primarily interested in those voices that are able to discern the link between their oppression and the historically oppressive religion(s) in their context that have rendered divine approval to that oppression. As such, indigenous deideologization looks upon with serious concern those indigenous voices that have bought into the divinely ordained nature of their suffering.

Therefore, indigenous deideologization implores the theologian to construct a theological method that speaks directly to the nuances of oppression in that theologian's context (Cone) using, specifically or in general, the hermeneutic circle (Segundo) as a means of: (1) bringing an ideological suspicion to the theologian's context while also recognizing that the will to oppress and to justify it on religious grounds is part of a larger ideological superstructure; (2) recognizing the link between inhuman treatment and an equally inhuman application of the dominant religion in that context and the close affinity of religious leaders and theologians with that application; and (3) developing a passionate critique of that oppressive application as well as liberative theological presuppositions that effectively refute those theological claims of the dominant group wherein the voices of indigenous peoples must play a significant role.

If indigenous deideologization is to be an effective method, four clearly distinct yet interrelated modes must emerge in its development: (1) a contextual mode, (2) a deideological mode, (3) a postmodern mode, and (4) a liberative mode.

Indigenous Deideologization as a Contextual Method

Indigenous deideologization takes seriously Douglas John Hall's dictum "Contextualization is the sine qua non of all theological reflection." Further, indigenous deideologization maintains that human suffering is contradictory to God's will and that those who are the victims of suffering are best qualified to speak to how God's revelation in Jesus liberates them from that suffering. Over the past three decades, we have seen significant changes in student enrollments in graduate programs in religion and theology. In increasing numbers, women and persons of color are pursuing studies in religious scholarship seeking to express their community's unique way of understanding God's activity in Jesus through formal theological reflection. We have witnessed the emergence of those developments in the form of Black, Womanist, Feminist, Mujerista, Latin American, and African theologies, as well as the emergence of liberation theology in England and Holland. Indigenous deideologization sees this as a necessary development in academic theology if theological reflection is going to be faithful to the scriptural witness and contribute to the resolution of contemporary problems.

For Cone, this means an exploration of the methodological question, "What has the gospel of Jesus to do with the struggle of black people to free themselves from white supremacy?" In this regard, the biblical witness is clear, for Cone, in confirming that the revelation of God is one of identification with the victims of oppression and not the powerful. Since, according to Cone, white theology has served as a divine sanction for black dehumanization, serving the interests of a racist white community, any relevant theological perspective that claims to speak of Jesus Christ must depart not from the community of the powerful but rather those who have been the victims of that power. Cone puts the matter more succinctly:

> Theology is always identified with a particular community. It is either identified with those who inflict oppression or with those who are its victims. A theology of the latter is authentic Christian theology and a theology of the former is a theology of the Antichrist. Insofar as black theology is a theology arising from an identification with the oppressed black community and seeks to interpret the gospel of Jesus in the light of the liberation of that community, it is Christian theology. American white theology is a theology of the Antichrist insofar as it arises from an identification with the white community, thereby placing God's approval on white oppression of black existence.[28]

In the effort to be ultimately contextual, Cone chose blackness as his principle of interpretation. Although such a principle seems, on the surface, more myopic than contextual, Cone, as stated in Chapter 2, speaks of both a physical blackness and an ontological blackness. Borrowing from Tillich's notion of the symbolic nature of all theological language, Cone maintains that blackness must be seen ultimately as a symbol that best represents what it means to be oppressed in America. The focus on blackness does not mean

---

[28] Cone, *A Black Theology of Liberation*, 6.

that only blacks suffer as victims in a racist society, but that blackness is an ontological symbol and a visible reality which best describes what oppression means in America.[29]

Thus, blackness is Cone's way of most clearly demonstrating the relevance of God's revelation to the contemporary situation in general and his community's understanding of God's activity in particular. The very existence of Black Theology is dependent on its ability to relate itself to the human situation unique to oppressed persons in general and blacks particularly.[30] This represents, for Cone, the significance of contextualization in theological reflection.

As for Segundo, the significance of contextualization is seen clearly in the title of one of his major works: *Our Idea of God*. Segundo uses the possessive pronoun "our" in referring to the poor of Latin America and its understanding of God's activity and in stark contrast to that of classical theology. Segundo is particularly concerned about theology's traditional treatment of God that has allowed "theologians to discourse on what God is in [Godself], independent of our life and history." This has led, in Segundo's judgment, to an image of God whose revelation is either purely speculative or involved in human affairs only in an individualistic way. For Segundo, this contributes most significantly to an understanding of God that desires passivity and quietism in humans relative to social change, in other words, to an understanding of a God more concerned about individual morality than human liberation. According to Segundo:

> There does exist an image of God that justifies privacy, the source of individualism. Faith is linked solely to one's personal salvation and to the dictates of an individualistic morality. It is the image of a God whose providence justifies passivity and resignation, of a God enshrined in devotions and sacramentals that lead to semifatalism. One says explicitly that all these things are to be avoided.[31]

This understanding of God represents, for Segundo, an attempt to attenuate efforts to subvert power structures that benefit from the existing situation by divorcing God's revelation from the efforts of the poor to liberate themselves. Our unjust society and our perverted idea of God are in close and terrible alliance.[32]

Segundo refers to this approach as "superficial" and opts instead for an understanding of God wherein God reveals Godself in and through the existence of the oppressed seeking to effectuate their liberation. That is to

---

[29] Ibid., 7.

[30] Ibid., 36.

[31] Juan Luis Segundo, *Our Idea of God*, trans. John Drury (Maryknoll, N.Y.: Orbis Books, 1974) 18.

[32] Ibid., 8.

say, Segundo maintains that God lets us know who God is as God speaks to us about our liberation. The superficial approach would cause us to lose the most essential point: that if Jesus' whole message speaks to us of our existence and its transformation, it must be because through it and only through it, we know what God is *in Godself.*[33] Thus, for Segundo, God's revelation and human liberation are synonymous and, because this liberation is multi-dimensional (though primarily sociopolitical), it should occupy our total concern. Segundo explains:

> Would it be too much to say that, in line with the facts, the center of divine revelation concerns [humanity]; and that God appears and shows [Godself] on the human horizon in the process of [humanity's] existence from within? Is not the *gospel,* that is, the good news—the only news that can truly be good for us because it concerns us totally?[34]

This means, for Segundo, that only by looking at the plight of the poor and analyzing the nuances of poverty in various contexts can we construct a Christian theology that most adequately reflects God's revelation in Jesus in our times.

Indigenous Deideologization as a Deideological Method

Inasmuch as indigenous deideologization sees religio-political ideologies to be the most potent weapon available to dominant classes in justifying the existing situation and further sees the destruction of the credibility of religio-political ideologies to be the key to human liberation, it accedes with Segundo's assertion that a theology has the potential to be most liberative when it is in a process of deideologization. Indigenous deideologization further asserts the necessity of bringing to the theological task an ideological suspicion that links oppressive treatment of one group over another with an equally oppressive religious expression by the dominant group.

For Cone, this link is clearly discerned in his works regarding white American Christianity and the pernicious effects that the ideologies emerging from it have had on black people. This is seen most prominently, by Cone, in white Christianity's eschatological teaching to blacks that their salvation is exclusively ethereal and is earned only through satisfactory toil in the slavocracy. According to Cone:

> Unfortunately, Christianity came to the black [people] through white oppressors that demanded that [they] reject [their] concern for this world as well as [their] blackness and affirm the next world and whiteness. The black intellectual community, however, with its emphasis on black identity, is be-

---

[33] Ibid., 6.
[34] Ibid.

coming increasingly suspicious of Christianity because the oppressor has used it as a means of stifling the oppressed concern for present inequities.[35]

Therefore, for Cone, our ideological suspicion must lead us into the thinking that a religious faith given to us by our enslaver is not likely to go far in liberating us.

This suspicion of Cone regarding white Christianity should also lead us to the conclusion that the white church is white Christianity's most visible representative. Cone asserts that through its historical support of the enslavement and segregation of black people, the white church has contributed more to a doctrine of white supremacy than a doctrine of human liberation. This is true, for Cone, not only for the white church itself but for its sponsored institutions as well. Cone puts it this way:

> It is a sad fact that the white church's involvement in slavery and racism in America simply cannot be overstated. It not only failed to preach the kerygmatic Word but maliciously contributed to the doctrine of white supremacy. Even today, all of the church's institutions—including its colleges and universities—reveal its white racist character.[36]

Therefore, according to Cone, we must be very suspicious about a white American theology and the schools and churches out of which it emerges that has either refused to make black humanity a theological issue or has divinely sanctioned black dehumanization. As such, Cone sees white theology as an ideology of the establishment inasmuch as it

> has served oppressors well. Throughout the history of this country, from the Puritans to the death-of-God theologians, the theological problems treated in white churches and theological schools are defined in such a manner that they are unrelated to the problem of being black in a white, racist society. By defining the problem of Christianity in isolation from the black condition, white theology becomes a theology of white oppressors, serving as a divine sanction from criminal acts committed against blacks.[37]

Thus, for Cone, given that the religio-political ideologies emerging out of white theology are geared toward the dehumanization of blacks, this is precisely where the process of deideologization begins for Black Theology. It begins with the voices of black people and their encounters with and resistance to white supremacy laying the cornerstone for a theological perspective that roots God's revelation in Jesus in a liberated black humanity. To be human in a condition of social oppression involves affirming that which the

---

[35] James H. Cone, *Black Theology and Black Power*, 20th Anniversary Edition (San Francisco: Harper & Row, 1989) 33.

[36] Ibid., 72.

[37] Cone, *Black Theology of Liberation*, 9.

oppressor regards as degrading.[38] The essence of the gospel of Christ stands or falls on the question of black humanity, and there is no way that a church or institution can be related to the gospel of Christ if it sponsors or tolerates racism in any form.[39] Since Cone demonstrates his understanding of the nuances of oppression in his context and their effect on black humanity, his starting point of the presupposition of a liberated black humanity makes his method one rooted in deideologization.

Like Cone, Segundo is also concerned about the role of academic theology and the Church in divinely legitimating human oppression. As stated earlier, Segundo sees the basis of this legitimation in academic theology and the Church's making faith and revelation divine absolutes divorced from social, cultural, and historical reality. Segundo refers to this deficiency as *the ideological infiltration of dogma.* Segundo uses the term "infiltration" to best describe what he understands to be a break in the history of the Church when the will of Christ was usurped by that of the dominant classes. According to Segundo: "We must be told that at a certain moment in history the Church stopped listening to the voice of Christ and began to listen to the voice of the ruling classes and their selfish interests. We need these seeming harmful hypotheses to wake us from our ideological slumber."[40] Indeed, that ideological slumber, for Segundo, is best seen in the Church's preoccupation with ecclesial concerns that do not begin to address the suffering of the oppressed. Thus, Segundo is ideologically suspicious about faith expressions that are metaphysical, universal, and/or ahistorical—none of which can liberatively relate the central figure of Christian faith who was a physical, particular, and historical being to our contemporary situation.

Segundo lifts up the sacraments and the question of their historical efficacy as an example. Because, for Segundo, the sacraments are presented in the Church in light of ecclesial tradition and not human liberation, he concludes that they are nothing more than "the image of an *ahistorical* sacramental efficacy." What does that mean? To the majority of Christians, it undoubtedly means that God is more interested in non-temporal things than in solutions for the historical problems that are cropping up.[41] This leads unfortunately, for Segundo, to two dangerous outcomes. First, the Church's espousing of an ahistorical faith leads those in the Church to conclude that Christianity has very little, if any, historical significance. The second outcome grows out of the first. If Christian faith has no historical value, then it can easily lead parishioners into the thinking (even the profound

---

[38] Ibid., 15.

[39] Ibid., 14.

[40] Juan Luis Segundo, *The Liberation of Theology,* trans. John Drury (Maryknoll, N.Y.: Orbis Books, 1976) 42.

[41] Ibid., 40–1.

conviction!) that frequent participation in unchanging ecclesial rituals is the essence of religious efficacy. Thus, by making ecclesial expression ahistorical, it severely compromises, in Segundo's judgment, religion's ability to impact historical reality. This, for Segundo, has not occurred by coincidence. It has been purposely sought after by dominant classes as a means of preserving its privileged status in society. According to Segundo:

> Is it by chance, then, that this conception and practice of the sacraments dovetails perfectly with the interests of the ruling classes and is one of the most powerful ideological factors in maintaining the status quo? Would it be too much to admit the fact that sacramental *theology* has been influenced more by unconscious social pressures than by the gospel message itself?[42]

This, in Segundo's view, confirms the break in the history of the Church mentioned above when ideology made its way into the faith usurping Christ's historical, liberative reign. Regarding Christian tradition, Segundo concludes that "at some point in theological tradition an alien element must have been inserted into it," given that, "the Christian sources do not present us with any concept of a religious efficacy that is vertical and ahistorical."

In this sense, Segundo maintains that these ideologies must be exposed as such and that the historicizing of Christian theology is imperative for its deideologization. Segundo reminds us that a liberating theology can no longer "drag out metaphysical or universal questions that have been handed down from generation to generation by long tradition. Thus simple logic tells us that only a Christian community that is keenly sensitive to history can provide the basis for such a liberative theology."[43] History then, according to Segundo, is the theological criterion that distinguishes "a theology of liberation from a conservative, academic theology."

Indigenous Deideologization as a Postmodern Method

Since indigenous deideologization is a method committed to making the voices of indigenous peoples in oppressed contexts significant in the doing of theology, a break with modernity was unavoidable. By modernity I mean that period in the history of theology that, up to the latter part of the twentieth century, made Europe and its thinkers the central location for substantive theological reflection. It was thought that these thinkers could not only theologize relevantly to their European context, but also that their perspectives were so universal they could speak relevantly to contexts outside Europe. The result was the emergence of theological perspectives that either did not address the plight of suffering peoples outside Europe or justified the status quo. As the fallacies of modernity became more apparent,

---

[42] Ibid., 41.
[43] Ibid., 40.

it called into being a shift in the doing of theology called postmodernism which gives the theologian unlimited flexibility in determining the sources with which to articulate his/her theological perspective. As such, it gave theologians dissatisfied with modernity the right to unseat Europe as the sole locus for valid theological reflection. In this sense, indigenous deideologization is a method firmly rooted in postmodernity. While it does not completely exclude European sources in the doing of theology, indigenous deideologization is primarily geared toward unearthing sources from within the cultural experiences of an oppressed community for the purpose of understanding the essence of that community's encounter with God.

For Cone, this means the construction of a Black Theology of liberation rooted in sources that emerge in the black community and questioning Europe's ability to define what the theological issues of the black community are. Regarding the relationship between traditional American theology and its dependence on Europe, Cone explains:

> If American theology is going to serve the needs of the Church by relating the gospel to the political, economic, and social situation in America, it must cut its adoring dependence upon Europe as the place to tell us what theology ought to be talking about. Some European theologians, like Barth and Bonhoeffer, may serve as examples of how to relate theology to life, but not in defining our major issues.[44]

This close affinity between American theology and Europe is one which Cone thinks that the oppressed in America should be suspicious of given the European origin of racism and its ubiquitous reality in American life. According to Cone:

> Modern racism is European in origin, and America has been its vigorous offspring. It is the white man who has sought to dehumanize others because of his feelings of superiority or for his economic advantage. Racism is so deeply embedded in this country that it is hard to imagine that any white man can escape it.[45]

The pervasive nature of racial bigotry in this country is so evident, for Cone, that he questions whether Europe or white America has the ability to theologize from the perspective of the poor without rendering tacit or outright approval to the oppression of black people. White culture is so fundamentally racist, for Cone, that he is not optimistic about white people's ability to transcend it and theologize in terms of black liberation. Thus what is needed, in Cone's judgment, is the construction of a Black Theology to be done by black people that is rooted in the indigenous experiences of black people. This means a theology built not only on the traditional sources of

[44] Cone, *Black Theology and Black Power,* 44.
[45] Ibid., 16.

Christian theology (revelation, Scripture, and tradition) but also on the black experience, black history, and black culture. These sources serve as the matrix out of which Cone relates the gospel of Jesus Christ to the pain and suffering of being black in a white racist country as well as reveals the black response to it, that is, the black prophetic radical tradition, the black Christian tradition, the accounts of slaves and the dual meanings and tales in which the slaves couched their liberative yearnings. Therefore, according to Cone, Black Theology departs from two interrelated poles that white culture prevents most white theologians from coming to terms with: the liberation of blacks and the revelation of Jesus Christ.

Indigenous deideologization embraces the postmodern shift in theological reflection in general and those indigenous voices that demonstrate their "usability in the black liberation struggle" in particular.

Segundo's theological method is also firmly rooted in the extant postmodern tradition. As stated earlier, Segundo's method arises out of what he considered academic theology's making faith and revelation ecclesial dogmas that are ahistorical in nature. While conceding that his theological method utilizes the tools of European social analysis (namely that of Marx), Segundo is also convinced that the perspectives of European theologians have not effectively addressed the concerns of the Latin American poor. For Segundo, relevant theological reflection entails two components: (1) a thorough social analysis of the problems unique to that context, and (2) lending an ear to the voices of the oppressed. This interrelationship between trained theologians and the voices of the Latin American poor is Segundo's primary concern in his article "Two Theologies of Liberation."[46] Segundo distinguishes between what he refers to as "two lines of theological reflection." The first line emerged from middle-class university students who employed intellectual tools to unmask ideologies in general used by repressive governments to justify the poverty of the majority of the population. This lead the students to a new way of understanding Christian faith that linked Christian conversion with a profound commitment to social justice. Having concluded that these ideologies extended to all of Latin American culture, "Christian students could do nothing except include *theology*—the understanding of Christian faith—in the ideological mechanisms structuring the whole of our culture." The students then formed an alliance with theologians who began to reflect on the virulent effects of ideologies on the economic status and mental psyche of the oppressed. From Christian students to theologians working with them, this ideological suspicion thus became

---

[46] This article was originally published in *The Month* 17 (October 1984) 321–7. It also appears in Alfred T. Hennelly, ed., *Liberation Theology: A Documentary History* (Maryknoll, N.Y.: Orbis Books, 1990) 353–66. I have taken my citations from the latter.

a source of a new vision about what theology should become and about how a theologian was supposed to work to unmask the anti-Christian elements hidden in a so-called Christian society.[47]

The second line of theological reflection of which Segundo speaks is the common people of Latin America whose voices were discovered in the seventies through popular movements but who have been active since the mid-fifties. These voices developed into small organizations and became known as basic ecclesial communities (CEBs). CEBs are small groups of Catholics, organized by lay persons, who meet regularly to reflect on both the religious and secular status of the community. These meetings also include the rituals of ecclesial tradition (prayer, worship, Bible study, etc.). More importantly, CEBs have also been highly impacted by Paulo Freire's notion of *conscientization*[48] wherein they are seeking to discover the real causes of their oppression "and of the urgent need to become active agents of their own destiny in seeking avenues to change."

Yet Segundo and other theologians of the first line (particularly Boff) are concerned about the efficacy of the second line. Segundo wonders whether they are able to forward ideas that will liberate the Latin American poor given their unlearned status and their possible (even probable) internalization of the ideologies of the ruling class. Unlearned and so incapable of utilizing developed tools of ideological suspicion in a culture considered impartial and the same for all social classes, poor and marginalized people were led by their culture to accept distorted and oppressive hidden elements which "justified" their situation, and, among all these elements, a distorted and oppressive theology.[49]

While Segundo leaves open the question of whether these two lines of doing theology are diametric opposites or dialectically interrelated, indigenous deideologization opts for the latter, maintaining that this tension is a productive one insofar as it includes the tools of formal theological reflection as well as the voices of indigenous peoples (while leaving open the possibility of critiquing those voices that have internalized ideologies). This tension would not likely have occurred if not for the emergence of a postmodern paradigm. Thus postmodernity has allowed the oppressed to empower themselves through telling their stories on their own terms.

Indigenous Deideologization as a Liberative Method

Above all, indigenous deideologization is a liberative method. That is to say, it seeks to remove all barriers in society that hinder the full participation

---

[47] Segundo, "Two Theologies of Liberation," 355.

[48] See Freire's treatment of *conscientization* in his classic, *Pedagogy of the Oppressed* (New York: Continuum, 1970).

[49] Segundo, "Two Theologies of Liberation," 355.

of human beings because of a distinguishing physical characteristic (race and/or gender) or economic status. Indigenous deideologization further sees as the key to effectuating that liberation the development of a new way of doing theology that addresses the enduring problem of religio-political ideologies in justifying human oppression. This new way of doing theology is made all the more significant given the importance placed on religion and religious language in virtually all oppressor-oppressed contexts. Thus, there becomes the need to "waken us from our ideological slumber," in the words of Segundo, and construct a Christian theology that seeks to effectively counter historically oppressive treatments of Christian faith that have equated God's revelation with human exploitation and enslavement.

For Cone and Black Theology, liberation occurs both in and beyond history. Historically, sociopolitical liberation from white supremacy, according to Cone, has always been an existential goal for African Americans. A representative number of slaves intuited that Christian faith and their enslavement were incompatible despite efforts of slaveholders to convince them otherwise. Cone sees this understanding of the black experience and Christian faith as the cornerstone of the pre-Plessy black church. The black church in America was founded on the belief that God condemned slavery and that Christian faith meant political emancipation.[50]

This understanding of God and Christian faith evolved into two important insights that would serve as catalysts for black liberation. First, if God condemns slavery then it meant that black people were justified in doing what was necessary to end it. In this sense, slaves were convinced that their liberating activity was a contemporary manifestation of God's revelation. But more importantly, this signaled to slaves that they were free to develop liberative strategies irrespective of white thought. Cone skillfully illuminates this understanding in his treatment of the relationship between the gospel and black power. Cone writes:

> Therefore, Black Power seeks not understanding but conflict; addresses blacks and not whites; seeks to develop black support, but not white good will. Black Power believes in the utter determination of blacks to be free and not in the good intentions of white society. It says: If blacks are liberated, it will be blacks themselves who will be doing the liberating, not whites.[51]

Because of a history in which whites completely determined black existence, reducing them to a state of powerlessness, the notion of freeing oneself from white supremacy regardless of white thinking is Cone's meaning of Black Power, and the reason it is inextricably bound with black liberation.

The second insight informing black liberation is that Christian freedom means political emancipation, confirming liberation's historical nature. This

---

[50] Cone, *A Black Theology of Liberation*, 35.
[51] Cone, *Black Theology and Black Power*, 16–17.

understanding of Christian freedom challenges white supremacist claims that black liberation is otherworldly and is obtained only by serving whites well on earth. Any view of liberation that fails to take seriously a people's freedom in history is not biblical and is thus unrelated to the One who has called us into being.[52]

Yet just as there is a liberation that occurs in history, for Cone, there is also a liberation that occurs beyond history. It is a history "not created by human hands," for Cone—one that transcends history.

> This simply means that the oppressed have a future not made with human hands but grounded in the liberating promises of God. They have a liberation not bound by their own strivings. In Jesus' death and resurrection, God freed us to fight against social and political structures while not being determined by them.[53]

Despite the implication, Cone does not understand this transhistorical liberation to be an opiate. Rather, he sees historical and transhistorical liberation as intersecting one another wherein the latter breaks in on the former, showing those who have been the victims of history that the eschatological promise of God will be realized as a future existential reality. Liberation as a future event is not simply *otherworldly* but is the divine future that breaks into their social existence, bestowing wholeness in the present situation of pain and suffering and enabling black people to know that the existing state of oppression contradicts their real humanity as defined by God's future.[54]

While indigenous deideologization accepts both historical and transhistorical liberation it is resolute in maintaining that historical liberation must take precedence to transhistorical liberation. Segundo reminds us that we must be mindful of attempts to water down the language of liberation or incorporate it into the status quo. If we were to treat liberation in terms that are more transhistorical it could sentence liberation theology to the same ahistorical irrelevance that we are trying so diligently to theologize away from.

As for Segundo, the hermeneutic circle is constructed for the purpose of bringing liberative potential to faith. Thus, while Cone is concerned about the content of liberation particularly in the black American context, Segundo wonders whether we can arrive at any meaningful understanding of liberation without first developing a method for removing those ideologies that keep us mired in a conservative, status quo–serving Christianity. Thus, Segundo's understanding of liberation is presupposed by the question, "How do we bring liberative potential to historically oppressive treatments of Christian faith?"

[52] Cone, *God of the Oppressed*, 153.
[53] Ibid., 158.
[54] Ibid., 159.

What has made this task far more formidable in recent times, for Segundo, is the fact that many religio-political ideologies have become so deeply entrenched in Christian tradition, they are being uncritically accepted as valid expressions of the faith. Christian tradition has brought a divine respectability to religio-political ideologies giving even greater credence to continue things as they are. This becomes apparent when looking at the phenomenon of Christian unity. Segundo is concerned that Christian unity has become a hollow unity, for it downplays the historical and cultural (and racial) differences of Christians in the attempt to accentuate their (so-called) common Christian conversion, that is, stressing the faith they have in common while failing to deal with the issues that divide them. Segundo puts it this way: "In short the Church must pay a high price for unity. It must say that the issues of suffering, violence, injustice, famine and death are less critical and decisive than religious formulas and rites."[55] This view of Christian unity is extremely problematic, for Segundo, in that it allows for the unity of "Christians" without differentiating the haves from the have-nots, the rich from the poor, and the colonizers from the colonized and in so doing severely hinders Christian faith's ability to effectuate historical liberation through the destruction of these relationships. The real problem of Christian unity comes down to this: When will we manage to break that conservative, oppressive, undifferentiated unity of Christians in order to establish an open dialogue with all those, be they Christians or not, who are committed to the historical liberation that should serve as the basis for the "service of reconciliation" in and through real justice?[56]

This means, for Segundo, that the Church is to understand itself as a vehicle of reconciliation, but not at the expense of forsaking historical liberation. Rather, reconciliation is to be understood as the attempt to bring humans together in the name of Christianity for the cause of human liberation in history and not simply as confessing "Christians" convinced that historical liberation is not a religious issue. Segundo explains:

> The church responds to such criticisms, of course, alluding to fundamental biblical principles. It points to the "service of reconciliation" that Christians are supposed to perform, according to Paul (2 Cor 5:18ff); it also points to the universal reconciliation that is supposed to come about from Christ's work (Col 1:20). But in the very process of alluding to these things it forgets that the final eschatological reconciliation mentioned in those very texts is supposed to come to pass in and through the liberation of human beings; that it is not the result of any pious blindness towards existing oppression today and the means to combat it. And one of those means, if not the principal

---

[55] Segundo, *The Liberation of Theology*, 42–3.
[56] Ibid., 44.

one, is to separate those suffering oppression from those who are its fo-
menters or accomplices.[57]

This means, for Segundo, that any aspect of Christian tradition or theology
that does not make the historical liberation of "the least of these" its raison
d'être is ideology and is far removed from the task and purpose for which
Christ has called us.

Further, given that the oppressed are affected by ideologies that are not
only theological but cover all disciplines of the ideological superstructure,
Segundo maintains that liberation also entails exposing ideologies in other
disciplines. Segundo explains it this way:

> It should be clear that the methodology of an ever more liberated and liber-
> ating theology is not an emotional sinecure. One cannot simply utter the
> word "liberation" and then link it up with the Scriptures in more or less slip-
> shod fashion. Neither is it an ingenuous approach that allows the theologian
> to take the easy way out that is often taken by academic theology. For it does
> not allow theologians to set aside the great problems of today on the pretext
> that they belong to other fields or disciplines. Instead it forces them to con-
> front the major problems of history, biology, evolution, social change, and so
> forth.[58]

Thus, as Cone's treatment moves from the historical to the transhistorical,
Segundo's treatment remains historical throughout and moves across the
spectrum of the ideological superstructure. That is to say, Cone's treatment
moves vertically from history to beyond history while Segundo's moves hori-
zontally to the various arenas of oppression and the justifications for it.

Conclusion

What I have tried to accomplish with this work has particular and general dimensions. Particularly, I have attempted to show that Cone's theological method is in the process of deideologization by demonstrating that
Cone constructed a theological method that completes Segundo's hermeneutic circle. As such, it demonstrates that Cone's theology is possessed of
deideological dimensions: bringing an ideological suspicion to theological
reflection presupposed by a recognition of the link between black oppression and historically oppressive treatments of Christianity by whites regarding black humanity. Cone was further able to unmask the church and
the academy's close affinity with power structures in their divine legitimation of the oppression of black people. But, most importantly, Cone sought
to destroy the credibility of these oppressive treatments of Christianity by
constructing new theological presuppositions rooted in black liberation

---

[57] Ibid.
[58] Ibid., 236.

wherein black strivings to liberate themselves from white supremacy are the contemporary revelation of God.

I have further tried to show the significance of Segundo's attempt to offer a lens through which we as liberation theologians can employ to critique our work, the hermeneutic circle, stressing the phenomenon of religio-political ideologies and their need to be deideologized as the most effective point of departure if theology is to make a decisive contribution to the realization of a liberated humanity. Some may consider my choice of Segundo's hermeneutic circle a sound choice and some may not. There are others who may think that it needs amending in areas other than the ones I expressed to be more relevant to their own contexts. If so, these decisions are left entirely to the discretion of the reader. For in Segundo's own words, "The challenge is not to do the same things as we are doing [in Latin America], for this would not make sense. But certainly it is to fight creatively for the same cause in your own context, with your own tools, and, above all, with your own hearts."

Generally, my intent was to reestablish the significance of religio-political ideologies in theological reflection and ideologies over the whole and their virulent effects on the social, economic, political, mental, moral, and spiritual well-being of both the oppressor and the oppressed. They sentence the former to an inflated, superior image of themselves which produces a mindset that equates their dehumanization of oppressed peoples with service to God. They produce in the latter a severely damaged self-image causing oppressed people to constantly struggle with their intellectual endowment, cultural expressions, aesthetic characteristics, and general self-worth. If Karl Barth's intent in *Der Romerbrief* was to rediscover revelation as the decisive category of theological reflection, my intent with this work is to reestablish religio-political ideologies as the necessary starting point for relevant theological reflection. While understanding that theology is speech about God, it should also be understood that it is speech emerging out of the culture of human beings. As such, only by thoroughly examining the cultural norms that determine how we as humans receive our revelations will we be able to faithfully put forth theological perspectives that are mutually beneficial to all segments of the human family.

To be sure, there is very little novelty involved in the issues I have raised given that there is nothing novel about racism, sexism, and classism, and the efforts to justify them as the natural order of things. Cone and Segundo have been struggling with these issues for at least three decades prior to this work and many others prior to them. Yet, my concern is not to be novel per se, but rather to be relevant. As a result, I am convinced that novelty does not always imply relevance. For novelty, in the interests of being "intellectually correct," has historically meant not departing from ideologies in theological reflection or worse yet theologizing from perspectives that do not link human liberation with God's revelation. However, such theological perspectives have not the vitality or substance to, in Martin Luther King's words, "feed hungry souls at midnight." I suspect that in the final analysis, when race, gender, and class antagonisms have taken their last breath, history will record that human liberation came not as a result of those who sought to transcend these issues in the name of intellectual creativity, but because of those who had the courage to continually revisit them.

Works Cited

Books by James H. Cone

Cone, James H. *A Black Theology of Liberation.* New York: Lippincott, 1970.
———. *The Spirituals and the Blues: An Interpretation.* New York: Seabury Press, 1972.
———. *God of the Oppressed.* San Francisco: Harper & Row, 1975.
———. *My Soul Looks Back.* Nashville: Abingdon, 1982.
———. *For My People.* Maryknoll, N.Y.: Orbis Books, 1984.
———. *Speaking the Truth: Ecumenism, Liberation and Black Theology.* Grand Rapids, Mich.: Eerdmans, 1986.
———. *Black Theology and Black Power.* Twentieth Anniversary Edition. San Francisco: Harper & Row, 1989.
———. *A Black Theology of Liberation.* Twentieth Anniversary Edition. Maryknoll, N.Y.: Orbis Books, 1990.
———. *Martin and Malcolm and America.* Maryknoll, N.Y.: Orbis Books, 1991.
Cone, James H., and Gayraud S. Wilmore, eds. *Black Theology: A Documentary History, 1966–1979.* Maryknoll, N.Y.: Orbis Books, 1979.
———. *Black Theology: A Documentary History, 1980–1992.* Maryknoll, N.Y.: Orbis Books, 1993.

Articles by James H. Cone

Cone, James H. "Black Power, Black Theology, and the Study of Theology and Ethics." *Theological Education* 6 (Spring 1970) 202–15.
———. "Freedom, History, and Hope." *The Journal of the Interdenominational Theological Center* 1 (Fall 1973) 55–64.
———. "Black Theology on Revolution, Violence, and Reconciliation." *Union Seminary Quarterly Review* 31:1 (Fall 1975) 5–14.
———. "Black Theology and Ideology: A Response to My Respondents." *Union Seminary Quarterly Review* 31:1 (Fall 1975) 71–86.
———. "The Content and Method of Black Theology." *The Journal of Religious Thought* 32 (Fall–Winter 1975) 90–103.
———. "Black Theology in American Religion." *Journal of the American Academy of Religion* 53:3 (December 1985) 755–71.

Publications of Juan Luis Segundo

Segundo, Juan Luis. *Grace and the Human Condition.* Trans. John Drury. Maryknoll, N.Y.: Orbis Books, 1973.

————. *Masas y Minorias en la dialectica divina de la liberacion.* Buenos Aires: Editorial la Aurora, 1973.

————. *Our Idea of God.* Trans. John Drury. Maryknoll, N.Y.: Orbis Books, 1974. Originally published by Carlos Lohle, Buenos Aires, 1970.

————. *The Liberation of Theology.* Trans. John Drury. Maryknoll, N.Y.: Orbis Books, 1976. Originally published by Carlos Lohle, Buenos Aires, 1975.

————. *Faith and Ideologies.* Trans. John Drury. Maryknoll, N.Y.: Orbis Books, 1984.

————. *The Historical Jesus of the Synoptics.* Trans. John Drury. Maryknoll, N.Y.: Orbis Books, 1985.

————. *The Liberation of Dogma: Faith, Revelation, and Dogmatic Teaching Authority.* Trans. Phillip Berryman. Maryknoll, N.Y.: Orbis Books, 1992.

————. *Signs of the Times: Theological Reflections.* Trans. Robert R. Barr. Maryknoll, N.Y.: Orbis Books, 1993.

General

Berger, Peter. *The Noise of Solemn Assemblies.* New York: Doubleday, 1961.

————. *The Sacred Canopy: Elements of a Sociological Theory of Religion.* New York: Doubleday, 1967.

Berger, Peter, and Thomas Luckmann. *The Social Construction of Reality: A Treatise in the Sociology of Knowledge.* New York: Doubleday, 1967.

Botkin, B. A., ed. *Lay My Burden Down: A Folk History of Slavery.* New York: Dell, 1973.

Buswell, James O., III. *Slavery, Segregation, and Scripture.* Grand Rapids, Mich.: Eerdmans, 1964.

Carlsnaes, Walter. *The Concept of Ideology and Political Analysis.* Westport, Conn.: Greenwood Press, 1981.

Chapman, Mark L. *Christianity on Trial.* Maryknoll, N.Y.: Orbis Books, 1996.

Coleman, Will. *Tribal Talk: Black Theology, Hermeneutics, and African/American Ways of "Telling the Story."* University Park: Pennsylvania State University Press, 2000.

Cone, Cecil W. *Identity Crisis in Black Theology.* Nashville: African Methodist Episcopal Church, 1975.

Cummings, George, C. L. *A Common Journey: Black Theology (USA) and Latin American Liberation Theology.* Maryknoll, N.Y.: Orbis Books, 1993.

Dussel, Enrique. *Philosophy of Liberation.* Maryknoll, N.Y.: Orbis Books, 1985.

Earl, Riggins R., Jr. *Dark Symbols, Obscure Signs: God, Self, and Community in the Slave Mind.* Maryknoll, N.Y.: Orbis Books, 1993.

Evans, James H., Jr. *We Have Been Believers: An African American Systematic Theology.* Minneapolis: Fortress Press, 1992.

Fanon, Frantz. *The Wretched of the Earth.* New York: Grove Press, 1965.

————. *Black Skins, White Masks.* New York: Grove Press, 1967.

Freire, Paulo. *Pedagogy of the Oppressed.* New York: Continuum, 1992.

Grant, Jacquelyn. *White Women's Christ and Black Women's Jesus: Feminist Christology and Womanist Response.* Atlanta: Scholars Press, 1989.

Haselden, Kyle. *The Racial Problem in Christian Perspective.* New York: Harper Publishers, 1959.

Holland, Joe, and Peter Henriot. *Social Analysis: Linking Faith and Justice.* Maryknoll, N.Y.: Orbis Books, 1985.

Hopkins, Dwight N. *Shoes that Fit Our Feet: Sources for a Constructive Black Theology.* Maryknoll, N.Y.: Orbis Books, 1993.

———. *Down, Up, and Over: Slave Religion and Black Theology.* Minneapolis: Fortress Press, 2000.

Hopkins, Dwight N., and George C. L. Cummings, eds. *Cut Loose Your Stammering Tongue: Black Theology in the Slave Narratives.* Maryknoll, N.Y.: Orbis Books, 1991.

Jones, William R. *Is God a White Racist?* 2nd ed. Boston: Beacon Press, 1998. Originally published in 1973.

———. "Theodicy and Methodology in Black Theology: A Critique of Washington, Cone, and Cleage." *Harvard Theological Review* 64 (1971).

Jordan, Winthrop. *White Over Black: American Attitudes Toward the Negro, 1550–1812.* Chapel Hill: University of North Carolina Press, 1968.

Kelsey, George. *Racism and the Christian Understanding of Man.* New York: Scribner, 1965.

Lincoln, C. Eric. *Race, Religion, and the Continuing American Dilemma.* New York: Hill & Wang, 1984.

Litwack, Leon F. *Been in the Storm So Long: The Aftermath of Slavery.* New York: Vintage Books, 1979.

Loescher, Frank Samuel. *The Protestant Church and the Negro: A Pattern of Segregation.* New York: Association Press, 1948.

Logan, Rayford W. *The Betrayal of the Negro.* New York: Macmillan, 1965.

Long, Charles H. "Structural Similarities and Dissimilarities in Black and African Theologies." *Journal of Religious Thought* 32:2 (Fall–Winter 1975).

Mannheim, Karl. *Ideology and Utopia: An Introduction to the Sociology of Knowledge.* New York: Harcourt, Brace and World, 1936.

Marx, Karl. *Kapital: A Critique of Political Economy.* New York: Kerr, 1906.

Marx, Karl, and Friedrich Engels. *The German Ideology.* London: Lawrence & Wishart, 1938.

———. *On Religion.* New York: Schocken Books, 1964.

———. *On Colonialism.* New York: International Publishers, 1982.

Morrison, Toni. *Beloved.* New York: Penguin Books, 1987.

Myrdal, Gunnar. *An American Dilemma.* 2 vols. New York: McGraw-Hill Book Company, 1944.

Niebuhr, H. Richard. *The Social Sources of Denominationalism.* New York: Meridian Books, 1929.

Niebuhr, Reinhold. *Moral Man and Immoral Society.* New York: Scribner, 1932.

Pinn, Anthony B. *Why Lord? Suffering and Evil in Black Theology.* New York: Continuum, 1995.

Quarles, Benjamin. *The Negro in the Making of America.* New York: Macmillan, 1969.

Raboteau, Albert. *Slave Religion: The "Invisible Institution" in the Antebellum South.* New York: Oxford University Press, 1978.

Roberts, J. Deotis. *Liberation and Reconciliation: A Black Theology.* Philadelphia: Westminster Press, 1971.

———. *Black Theology Today: Liberation and Contextualization.* New York: E. Mellen Press, 1983.

Schüssler Fiorenza, Elisabèth. *Bread Not Stone: The Challenge of Feminist Biblical Interpretation.* Boston: Beacon Press, 1984.

Serequeberhan, Tsenay, ed. *African Philosophy: The Essential Readings.* New York: Paragon House, 1991.

Smith, H. Shelton. *In His Image, but . . . Racism in Southern Religion, 1780–1910.* Durham, N.C.: Duke University Press, 1972.

Stampp, Kenneth M. *The Peculiar Institution: Slavery in the Ante-Bellum South.* New York: Vintage Books, 1956.

Stark, Werner. *The Sociology of Knowledge.* London: Routledge and Kegan Paul, 1958.

Thurman, Howard. *Jesus and the Disinherited.* New York: Abingdon-Cokesbury Press, 1949.

Tucker, Robert C. *The Marx-Engels Reader.* W. W. Norton & Company, 1978.

Walker, David. *David Walker's Appeal.* Baltimore: Black Classic Press, 1993.

Washington, Joseph R. *The Politics of God.* Boston: Beacon Press, 1967.

———. *Race and Religion in the Early Nineteenth Century America, 1800–1850: Constitution, Conscience, and Calvinist Compromise.* 2 vols. Lewiston, N.Y.: E. Mellen Press, 1984.

———. *Race and Religion in the Mid-Nineteenth Century America, 1850–1877: Protestant Parochial Philanthropists.* 2 vols. Lewiston, N.Y.: E. Mellen Press, 1989.

West, Cornel. *Prophesy Deliverance! An Afro-American Revolutionary Christianity.* Philadelphia: Westminster Press, 1982.

Williams, Delores S. *Sisters in the Wilderness: The Challenge of Womanist God-Talk.* Maryknoll, N.Y.: Orbis Books, 1993.

Wilmore, Gayraud S. *Black Religion and Black Radicalism: An Interpretation of the Religious History of Afro-American People,* 2nd ed. Maryknoll, N.Y.: Orbis Books, 1983.

Woodward, C. Vann. *The Strange Career of Jim Crow.* New York: Oxford University Press, 1966.

Index of Subjects

The entries followed by an asterisk (*) refer specifically to the theology of James H. Cone; those followed by two asterisks (**) refer specifically to the theology of Juan Luis Segundo.